Zoology

for Kids

WITH 21 ACTIVITIES

UNDERSTANDING AND WORKING WITH ANIMALS

Josh *and* Bethanie Hestermann

CHICAGO REVIEW PRESS

© 2015 by Josh Hestermann and Bethanie Hestermann
Foreword © 2015 by Martin Kratt and Chris Kratt
All rights reserved
First edition
Published by Chicago Review Press, Incorporated
814 North Franklin Street
Chicago, Illinois 60610
ISBN 978-1-61374-961-6

Library of Congress Cataloging-in-Publication Data
Hestermann, Josh, 1983–
  Zoology for kids : understanding and working
with animals : with 21 activities / Josh and Bethanie
Hestermann. — First edition.
      pages cm
  Includes bibliographical references and index.
  Audience: Ages 9 and up.
  ISBN 978-1-61374-961-6
  1. Zoology—Juvenile literature. 2. Zoology—Study
and teaching—Activity programs. 3. Zoology—
Vocational guidance—Juvenile literature.
  I. Hestermann, Bethanie, 1986– II. Title.

  QL49.H54 2015
  590—dc23

                              2014042745

Cover and interior design: Sarah Olson
Cover images: (front cover top, left to right) penguin
exhibit, courtesy of ZSL London Zoo; koala, courtesy of
Tampa's Lowry Park Zoo / Dave Parkinson; clownfish and
an angelfish, © istock.com / 101cats; bottle feeding a baby
addax antelope, courtesy of Chicago Zoological Society /
Jim Schulz; pygmy marmoset, © istock.com / GlobalP;
(front cover bottom, left to right) zebra, courtesy of Mark
Gonka; boy with salamander, © istock.com / MissHibiscus;
butterfly, courtesy of Chicago Zoological Society / Jim
Schulz; polar bear exhibit, courtesy of Chicago Zoological
Society / Jim Schulz; (back cover, left to right) poison dart
frog, courtesy of Chicago Zoological Society / Jim Schulz;
western lowland gorilla, courtesy of ZSL London Zoo; bird
of paradise, courtesy of Woodland Park Zoo / Dennis Dow
Activity illustrations: Jim Spence

Printed in the United States of America
5 4 3 2 1

In loving memory of Sheren Clements.

photo: authors' collection

Contents

Foreword by the Kratt Brothers · v

Authors' Notes · vi

Time Line · viii

Introduction: What is Zoology? · 1

Part 1

ZOOLOGY FOR BEGINNERS · 5

1 Animals—Form and Function · 7

Bake an Edible Animal Cell · 11

Dig Up "Animal Bones" · 15

Play the Dolphin Echolocation
   Game · 18

Explore Concealing Coloration · 22

2 Understanding Animal Behavior · 25

Test Your Sense of Direction · 29

Demonstrate a Butterfly's Life Cycle · 34

Communicate Like a Deep-Sea
   Animal · 38

3 Animals and Their Environments · 41

Eat a Bat Fruit Salad · 45

Construct a Food Chain · 48

Part 2

WORKING ON THE WILD SIDE—ZOOLOGY IN REAL LIFE · 51

4 Zookeepers, Aquarists, and Other Zoo Crew · 53

Create Behavioral Enrichment · 59

Train Your Friends · 62

Plan and Draw an Exhibit · 65

5 Call the Doctor! Veterinarians · 69

Mold Tiger Teeth · 72

Vital Signs, Part 1: Build a
   Stethoscope · 78

Vital Signs, Part 2: Take Your Vitals · 82

6 Wildlife Researchers · 85

Conduct an Experiment:
   Keeping Warm · 90

Backyard Zoology: Perform Field
   Research · 95

Invent a New Species · 98

7 Conservation Warriors · 101

Survive Habitat Loss:
   The Resource Game · 106

Make an Endangered Species
   Flyer · 111

Interview a Zoologist · 112

Acknowledgments · 115

Glossary · 117

Resources · 121

Selected Bibliography · 123

Index · 125

FOREWORD

Calling all creature-crazy kids!

There's so much to learn about animals, and this book, *Zoology for Kids*, is a great way for you and all of your animal-loving friends to jump right into the world of zoology.

Animals are all around us, and that means that the science of zoology is right there for you to study—any day and any time you see an animal! Ever since we were kids, we've been fascinated by cool creatures, and we started creature adventuring in our very own backyard. Today, we spend our time traveling the world, learning more about our fellow creatures, and sharing what we learn with kids just like you. We hope you get started on your own personal study of zoology by trying the fun and eye-opening activities in this book.

Use *Zoology for Kids* as a resource to learn as much as you can, then share what you've learned with all your friends. Follow your dreams and soon enough, you'll be having creature adventures around your neighborhood today—and around the world tomorrow!

Keep on creature adventuring, and we'll see you on the creature trail!

Your friends,
MARTIN KRATT AND CHRIS KRATT
Creators and stars of *Zoboomafoo* and *Wild Kratts*

AUTHORS' NOTES

My journey as a zoologist began when I was just 11 years old. At the time, I didn't even know what a zoologist was! I remember taking a trip across the country from my home state of Arizona to the Midwest to visit Chicago's Brookfield Zoo. It was during this trip that I first told my mom I wanted to work with animals when I grew up. I never gave up on that dream.

Pursuing a career as a zoologist is hard work! There are lots of people who love animals and want to make a career out of working with them. It was thanks to several years of dedication and support from my family and friends that I "made it." I've worked with some wonderful animals along the way—from giraffe, wallabies, and lemurs to parrots, alligators, and pythons. I even had the privilege of working at Brookfield Zoo, the very same place I visited when I was just 11 years old. While there, I helped take care of bottlenose dolphins, gray seals, harbor seals, and my favorite animals—California sea lions. Today, I get to go to work every day at the Aquarium of the Pacific, where I take care of sea lions, harbor seals, sea otters, penguins, and other species.

Over the years I've also worked with hundreds of talented zoologists who love animals, just like me. Every day, kids like you come up to me and ask what it takes to be a zoologist. I can't help but smile and remember it wasn't so long ago that I was in your shoes. My wife, Bethanie, and I decided to write this book because we think there is so much beauty in the world and it's important to understand, respect, appreciate, and enjoy it. Since we also share a love for education and learning, we put our heads together to create *Zoology for Kids*.

As you read this book, we hope it helps you feel more connected with the animal kingdom. You will learn the ins and outs of zoology, but most of all, you will learn what you can do to be part of this community—a community that works every day to preserve and protect this amazing world we call home.

—Josh Hestermann, coauthor

Growing up in my family meant hiking through deserts and canyons, pitching a tent and camping high up in the mountains, and even riding waves on the California coast. When I was outside, I felt happy and free. I didn't know it then, but my appreciation for the natural world was the beginning of my journey as a zoologist.

Then, I married a zookeeper. Josh's love for animals and my love for natural places went together like a fruit bat and a fig tree. (Don't get that comparison yet? You will!) In other words, we made a good team. Together, we more fully began to understand the unique and complicated relationship humans have with the other animals that share Planet Earth.

As a writer, I am living proof that no matter what your talents are, you can find a way to participate in and contribute to the zoology community. Through *Zoology for Kids*, Josh and I hope to not only encourage your curious mind but to inspire

you to go for it—whatever "it" is for you. Whether you're a budding scientist, an amateur photographer, or a young poet, use your strengths to showcase what you love, to educate others, and to make a difference.

—Bethanie Hestermann, coauthor

Bethanie and Josh Hestermann pose with Zuma, a male California sea lion. *Courtesy of Mark Gonka*

Time Line

350 BC
Aristotle, the Father of Zoology, writes *The History of Animals*

AD 77 (*circa*)
Pliny the Elder completes *Natural History*

AD 400 (*circa*)
Polynesians settle on Easter Island

1551
Conrad Gesner publishes first volume of *Historiae animalium*, an early animal encyclopedia

1628
William Harvey describes the circulation of blood in animals

1665
Robert Hooke first uses the term *cell*

1681
The dodo, a flightless bird species, becomes extinct

1683
Anton van Leeuwenhoek observes and describes bacteria

1750 (*circa*)
Carolus Linnaeus develops system for naming animal species

1752
Schönbrunn Menagerie (today Schönbrunn Zoo) opens in Vienna, Austria

1826
Zoological Society of London is founded

1828
London Zoo in London, England, opens to scientific fellows

1831–1836
HMS *Beagle*'s second voyage with Charles Darwin on board

1833
Louis Agassiz studies extinct life, publishes research on fish fossils

1838
John James Audubon finishes publishing *The Birds of America*

1846
London Zoo opens to the paying public

1853
London Zoo Aquarium opens in London, England

1856
Aquarium opens at Barnum's American Museum in New York City (it will burn down in 1865)

1858
Rudolf Virchow proposes that every cell comes from a preexisting cell

1859
Charles Darwin describes natural selection in *Origin of Species*

1859
Philadelphia Zoo in Philadelphia, Pennsylvania, is incorporated (it will open in 1874)

1860–1863
Boston Aquarial and Zoological Gardens is open to the public

1860 (*circa*)
Louis Pasteur begins studying bacteria and infectious diseases; later develops first vaccines

1865
Gregor Mendel presents law of inheritance and lays groundwork for study of genetics

1872–1876
HMS *Challenger* expedition offers unprecedented exploration of the ocean

1873
National Aquarium opens in Woods Hole, Massachusetts (later moves to Washington, DC)

1900 (*circa*)
Ivan Pavlov studies and demonstrates how animals learn

1914
The last passenger pigeon dies and the species becomes extinct

1938
B. F. Skinner publishes *The Behavior of Organisms*

1940
Roger Arliner Young becomes first African American woman to receive a PhD in zoology

1951
Rachel Carson publishes *The Sea Around Us*, a bestseller celebrating the natural world

1969
Robert Paine coins the term *keystone species*

1973
Konrad Lorenz and Nikolaas Tinbergen's work in animal behavior earns Nobel Prize for Physiology or Medicine

1981
The Association of Zoos and Aquariums launches Species Survival Plan program

1985
Edward O. Wilson develops concept of biodiversity

1991 (*circa*)
Efforts begin to reintroduce black-footed ferrets into their native habitat

2009 (*circa*)
Excavations reveal ancient zoo in Hierakonpolis, Egypt

2012
Monterey Bay Aquarium Research Institute discovers the harp sponge

2013
Smithsonian scientists discover the olinguito

Courtesy of Woodland Park Zoo / Dennis Dow

Introduction

WHAT IS ZOOLOGY?

nimals are *amazing*. They soar high above us, dive deep below us, and survive in Earth's most unlikely places. They swing among the treetops, scale rocky cliff faces, and burrow tunnels beneath the ground. Animals are *diverse*. Some are tiny, like the poison dart frog, which is barely bigger than a paperclip. Others are massive, like the blue whale—an underwater giant whose tongue weighs as much as an elephant!

Animals are *beautiful*. Some have vibrantly colored feathers or skin that changes color to match the surroundings. Others have shimmery scales, velvety fur, or sturdy patterned shells.

Animals are *mysterious*. They squeak, squawk, screech, grumble, growl, and roar. They fight, play, sing, and dance, and some of them even show off.

With all of this variety, it's no wonder we are fascinated by the animal kingdom. Our curiosity for the natural world fuels **zoology**, the study of animal life. This book, *Zoology for Kids*, aims to do two things. First, in part 1, it introduces some basics of zoology. Begin in chapter 1 by learning what animals are. Try

A Mandarin duck with beautifully bright feathers.
Courtesy of Tampa's Lowry Park Zoo / Dave Parkinson

(left) A toxic poison dart frog with sapphire-blue skin.
Courtesy of Chicago Zoological Society / Jim Schulz

(right) A close-up of a grapeshot carpet anemone.
© *Shedd Aquarium / Brenna Hernandez*

not to get hung up on big words and be sure to check the glossary or a dictionary if you get stumped. Stick with it, and in chapter 2, you'll learn about some of the amazing (and sometimes silly) things animals do. In chapter 3, you'll take a look at animals in their natural **habitats** and learn how they interact with each other and with their environments. Then, in part 2, it all comes together. You will see how real zoologists use this information every day by diving into the worlds of zookeepers and aquarists, veterinarians, wildlife researchers, and conservationists.

Along the way, you will meet some fascinating animals and the people who are passionate about them. You'll even get the chance to learn some new skills. Each chapter includes hands-on zoology-based activities to help you explore and discover this new world. You'll bake an edible animal cell, learn how to "train" your friends, sculpt a tiger's jawbone, invent a new species, and much more!

Zoology for Kids also offers practical advice for those looking to turn their passion into a career. There are many different ways to be part of the zoology community. For hands-on work with animals, you might become a zookeeper, an aquarist, or a veterinarian. If you love science, you might consider becoming a wildlife researcher or an **ecology** professor. Nature lovers might prefer one of many careers that work toward promoting **conservation**.

See a bolded word? Check the glossary for a definition.

No two zoologists are exactly alike, but each member of the zoology community has at least one thing in common: a special love and respect for the animal kingdom. Are you ready to begin your journey as a zoologist?

PART 1

Zoology for Beginners

"Animals differ from one another in their modes of subsistence, in their actions, in their habits, and in their parts."

—Aristotle, *The History of Animals*
(trans. D'Arcy Wentworth Thompson)

An African elephant.
Courtesy of DC Wagner / Nyaminyami Photography, LLC

ANIMALS—
FORM AND FUNCTION

It's late spring off the coast of Australia. A crab scuffles along the sandy seafloor surrounding a vibrant coral-reef community. It must be on guard. In the ocean, there are **predators** in every corner, looking for their next meal. A giant Australian cuttlefish lurks nearby. Its normally smooth skin has become textured, almost spiky. Its special skin cells have shifted to blue-gray and greenish-gold, mimicking the pattern of the reef over which the cuttlefish hungrily hovers. It has transformed itself into a near-perfect copy of the reef to its left and right. If you look closely enough, you might see two W-shaped pupils, watching . . . waiting.

Whoosh! Suddenly, the crab is snatched from behind. It wiggles and squirms, but two suctioned tentacles have exploded from the cuttlefish's beak, latching onto the crab and pulling it into its mouth. This time around, the crab has been outwitted. It walked right into the cuttlefish's trap.

The giant Australian cuttlefish is a magnificent creature, but so is the crab that ended up on its menu. Each animal is unique and valuable to its **ecosystem**,

The giant Australian cuttlefish is a master of disguise.
Courtesy of Roger Hanlon

A giant Australian cuttlefish can quickly disappear into the scenery thanks to its specialized skin cells.
Courtesy of Roger Hanlon

What Is an Animal?

If you have a sheet of paper nearby, make a list of the first 10 animals that come to mind. Now take a look at your list and try to answer this question: What is an animal? For instance, what makes a house cat an animal? Is it the fact that it has four legs, a fuzzy coat of fur, whiskers, and a tail? Not all animals can be described the same way. A hummingbird is an animal, but it has wings, feathers,

which makes studying zoology full of delights and surprises.

and a beak. Now take a look in a mirror. Humans are part of the animal kingdom, but we are quite different from hummingbirds and house cats.

So what do humans, house cats, and hummingbirds have in common that makes us different from, say, an oak tree or a tulip? It's not the fact that we're alive, because not all living things are animals. For instance, plants are living things, but plants are not animals. How do scientists know? Plants are **producers**; they create their own energy. Animals, on the other hand, like you and me and house cats, are **consumers**. Consumers can't make their own energy; they have to consume it. Humans are consumers because we get energy by eating producers (plants like fruits and veggies) and other consumers (animals like cows, pigs, and chickens).

Mobility, the ability to move around freely, is another characteristic of most animals. Whether they walk, hop, fly, slither, or swim, animals can typically travel from one place to another without any help. But when was the last time you saw an oak tree hop around the park? While some plants can move, like when a sunflower bends toward the sun, a plant can't get up and walk to the other end of the garden.

Some underwater animals are not mobile, such as adult sea squirts, but this is not the norm. Once they grow up, sea squirts permanently latch on to surfaces such as an ocean pier, a ship's hull, a rock, or even a large crab.

Animals' **cells**, the basic building blocks of life, are another distinguishing feature. Animal cells are made up of three basic parts: the plasma

The Father of Zoology and His Famous Pupil

The first zoologist—an ancient Greek philosopher named Aristotle—lived more than 2,000 years ago, from 384 to 322 BC. As legend would have it, Aristotle became the "Father of Zoology" with some help from his famous student, Alexander the Great, who was one of the most well-known military leaders of all time.

Aristotle was an important intellectual in his day. He was an expert in many subjects, including biology, history, and philosophy. King Philip II of Macedonia recognized Aristotle's influence and invited him to tutor his 13-year-old son, Alexander. Aristotle and Alexander worked together for a few years exploring their mutual interests in philosophy, science, and literature.

When Alexander became king in 336 BC, he began conquering neighboring lands. Alexander's conquest missions brought him and his army to new places filled with plants and animals they had never seen before. Years later, a Roman scholar named Pliny the Elder wrote that Alexander was so fascinated by these exotic species that he sent some of them back home to Aristotle, his former tutor.

Meanwhile, Aristotle had established a school in Athens after Alexander joined the military. He was not only a great teacher but also a student of the natural world. Aristotle's detailed observations about animals' forms, functions, and behaviors were the first of their kind. His work in zoology continued to influence the scientific community for hundreds of years after his death. Could Alexander the Great's conquests have helped Aristotle in his quest to understand and document the natural world, as legend suggests? We will never know for sure.

Humans, house cats, and hummingbirds are all animals. What do these species have in common?
Courtesy of Jeffrey B. Vrieling

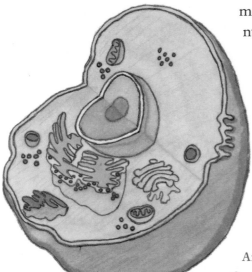

Animal cell.
Courtesy of Jeffrey R. Vrieling

membrane (the thin border around a cell), the nucleus (the control center of a cell), and the cytoplasm (the "stuff" or matter within a cell). Plant cells are different because they have an extra part, a more rigid border called a cell wall.

Cells vary in size, but each one is so small, you can only see it with the help of a microscope. If you were to take a really close-up look, you'd see how complex and impressive a tiny animal cell really is.

Animals' Forms

When similar cells group together, they form **tissues**. Tissues make up organs like the heart, brain, and lungs. All animals have similar cells, but not all animals have the same types of tissues. For instance, some animals that live in the sea, such as fish, have gills—organs that make it possible for them to breathe oxygen underwater. Other animals, such as land animals and marine mammals, have lungs—organs that make it possible for them to breathe oxygen from the air.

Organs help an animal's body perform basic functions that keep it alive. Gills and lungs allow

Animal Cell Lingo

There's a lot going on inside the cells in an animal's body. In fact, there's so much going on that scientists need many specialized terms to describe all of it. Here are just a few of them.

Within each cell are tiny structures called organelles. Each organelle has a job that helps the cell function. Ribosomes, for instance, help create protein molecules. Proteins have several jobs that help keep an animal alive, such as transporting oxygen. Other organelles, like mitochondria, help create energy for the cell. You can think of mitochondria as miniature power generators.

Animal cells also contain endoplasmic reticulum, which looks like a flat noodle that has been folded several times. When free ribosomes attach to the endoplasmic reticulum, it's considered "rough." If there are no ribosomes attached, it's considered "smooth." Rough and smooth endoplasmic reticula work with other organelles like Golgi bodies to circulate material throughout the cell. Meanwhile, lysosomes help keep the cell healthy by breaking down or digesting unneeded materials.

Near the center of an animal cell is its nucleus. A nucleus is like the director of a play. It keeps tabs on all the cell's actors—the organelles—and makes sure performances run smoothly. The nucleus also stores chromosomes. Chromosomes store information that distinguishes one species from another, and one individual animal from another. There is much more to learn about cellular biology, but now that you have a basic understanding, test your knowledge by baking an edible animal cell.

Bake an Edible Animal Cell

Animals' cells are the most basic way they differ from other living organisms such as plants. Use what you've learned about animal cells to build a model out of food. When you're done, you can eat it!

ADULT SUPERVISION REQUIRED

INGREDIENTS

- Package of cake mix, any flavor (depending on the brand, you may also need eggs and oil)
- Vanilla frosting
- Tube of cake-decorating frosting, any color
- Peanut butter cup
- 5 gummy worms
- Container of sprinkles, any shape and color
- 1 piece pull-and-peel licorice
- 3 Tootsie Rolls
- Small package of Skittles or M&Ms

UTENSILS

- Wooden spoon
- Large mixing bowl
- 9-inch round cake pan
- Wax paper
- Spatula or plastic knife

Preheat the oven, mix together the cake ingredients, and bake, following the directions on the package. After the cake is baked and cooled, remove it from the pan and place it on a flat surface covered in wax paper. Using a spatula or a plastic knife, cover the top of your animal cell with vanilla frosting.

The frosting represents the cell's cytoplasm. Next, use a tube of colored cake-decorating frosting to draw a circle along the outer edge of the cell. This colored line represents the plasma membrane—the outer boundary of an animal cell.

Unwrap the peanut butter cup and place it somewhere near the center of the cake. This represents the cell's nucleus.

Next, add the organelles. Place several gummy worms on the cake so they surround the nucleus. The gummy worms represent the endoplasmic reticulum. Add some sprinkles (ribosomes) between some of the gummy worms to create rough endoplasmic reticulum. The gummy

continued . . .

Bake an Edible Animal Cell, *continued*

worms without sprinkles represent smooth endoplasmic reticulum. Scatter some more sprinkles on your cake to represent free ribosomes.

To create a Golgi body, peel a strip from your piece of pull-and-peel licorice, fold it several times so it looks like an S, and place it within the cytoplasm.

Next, add the Tootsie Rolls to represent mitochondrion. To represent lysosomes, pick out a few Skittles or M&Ms of the same color and add them to the cytoplasm.

When you're done, show off your cake as you explain which part of an animal cell each piece of candy represents. Then, enjoy your creation. Bon appétit!

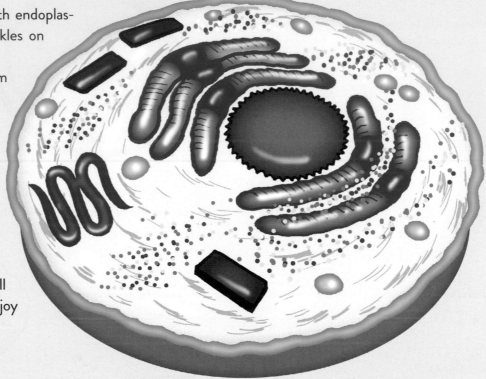

Extra Credit

Plant cells are more rectangular in shape than animal cells. They have a rigid cell wall as well as a plasma membrane, and they also have some different organelles, such as chloroplasts and a large vacuole. Research plant cells, then build an edible model to compare and contrast with your animal cell.

animals to inhale oxygen and exhale carbon dioxide. Organs like the stomach are part of an animal's digestive system, which is how animals get energy from their food. Other organs, such as the liver and kidneys, also work behind the scenes to support animal life.

Structural tissues help define the shape of an animal's body. These types of tissues include muscle, cartilage, and bone. Some animals, such as humans, have all three types. If you flex your arm, you can feel muscle tissue beneath your skin responding to the flex. If you touch your nose or ear, you can feel cartilage, a more flexible type of tissue that also makes up shark skeletons. Bone is a third type of structural tissue that makes up many animal skeletons, including yours.

When you think about skeletons, you may assume they always exist *inside* the body like human skeletons do. In reality, you can find three different types of skeletons within the animal kingdom. Humans have endoskeletons that support the body from the inside. Endoskeletons are usually made of bone or cartilage.

A second type of skeleton is called an exoskeleton, which exists *outside* an animal's body. Exoskeletons are strong structures that enclose the body of animals such as beetles and lobsters. Unlike endoskeletons, exoskeletons do not grow with the animal and must often be shed and regrown as the animal gets bigger.

A hydrostatic skeleton relies on internal pressure from body fluids for support. An earthworm has no bones, and yet it's strong enough to burrow through the earth. Animals with hydrostatic skeletons, such as earthworms, have special muscles that control internal pressure and keep their bodies inflated, kind of like a water balloon.

When it comes to animals' forms, there is some amazing diversity. But more often than not, animals have something in common: symmetry. If you were to draw an imaginary line down the center of a butterfly, you'd notice that the shapes, patterns, and colors you see on the right side are the same as the shapes, patterns, and colors on the left side. Other animals' bodies form a circle, such as sea anemones. Animals with this type of symmetry resemble a wheel, often with a mouth at the center.

Insects like this mantispid have exoskeletons.
Courtesy of Daniela Schmieder

Surviving in the Wild

Animals have many tools in their biological tool kit when it comes to survival. In fact, one of the most interesting reasons to study zoology is to learn how animals' forms help them survive against extreme temperatures, fierce predators, and other hurdles they face in their daily lives. Whether they have dense, waterproof fur or the ability to see in the dark, many animals simply wouldn't make it without their bodies' natural survival kits.

Your body has a natural survival kit, too. Have you ever noticed the ways your body reacts to outside temperatures? If it's hot, you might start sweating, which is your body's attempt to cool itself down. If it's cold, you might shiver, which is

Studying Ancient Animal Bones

Knowledge about animal skeletons is particularly important to paleontologists, scientists who study plants and animals of the past by analyzing **fossils**. In some cases, paleontologists work alongside archaeologists (scientists who study human **artifacts** and remains) to piece together the stories of ancient civilizations.

Imagine digging in the ground at an archaeological site and coming across the bones of some animals that were not native to the area. This is what happened to a team of archaeologists led by Renée Friedman while they were excavating near the ancient Egyptian city of Hierakonpolis.

Archaeologists believe Hierakonpolis, the City of the Hawk, was one of Egypt's earliest and largest cities along the Nile River, built a thousand years before the great Egyptian pyramids. In the site's elite cemetery, Renée's team uncovered the remains of more than 100 animals, including a leopard, two African elephants, two crocodiles, three hippos, and 15 baboons.

Why were these animals there? A closer look at the fossils may provide a clue. Some of the animals buried at Hierakonpolis had fractured bones that had healed before death. Because such injuries would have been fatal in the wild, archaeologists believe humans were tending to these animals' injuries. Many of the animals' preserved teeth also showed signs of abnormal wear, suggesting they were not eating a natural diet while they were alive.

These discoveries may suggest that in life, the animals were part of an ancient zoo. They were being fed and tended by human caretakers. It's likely the animals were brought to Hierakonpolis by the city's ruling elite to demonstrate their wealth and authority.

Archaeologists who have studied the animal remains buried at Hierakonpolis, like this baboon skeleton, believe there was an ancient zoo in this early Egyptian city.
Courtesy of Hierakonpolis Expedition / Renée Friedman

Dig Up "Animal Bones"

Imagine you are a paleontologist who is digging at the site of an ancient zoo. Your job is to find bone fragments and piece them together to help determine which type of animal was buried there.

MATERIALS

- Newspapers or paper towels
- Pen
- 3 craft sticks
- 8½-inch-by-11-inch foam sheet (available at craft stores)
- Scissors
- Small, round object (bottle cap, gumball, eraser, marble, rock, etc.)
- Markers
- Notebook paper
- Shoebox with no holes (or cover existing holes with duct tape)
- 12 cups of potting soil or dirt
- Spoon

Begin by covering your workspace with newspapers or paper towels. Trace three craft sticks onto a foam sheet and cut them out.

Next, use the foam cutouts to build an animal skeleton. Place one foam piece horizontally in front of you to act as the animal's spine. Cut the remaining two foam pieces in half. These four shorter pieces represent the animal's two front legs and two back legs.

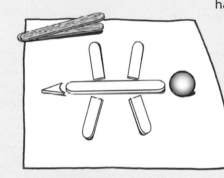

Find a small, round object and place it at one end of the spine for a skull. Cut off a small piece of foam from your scrap to use as a tail. Place the tailbone at the opposite end of the spine from the skull.

Use markers to make each bone a different color. For instance, make the spine purple, the front left leg green, the front right leg blue, the back left leg red, the back right leg yellow, and the tail black. Make sure to color both sides of each bone.

continued . . .

Dig Up "Animal Bones," *continued*

Arrange the skeleton on your workspace so each bone is where it should be. Write down which color you used for each bone.

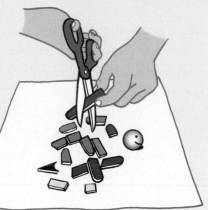

Cut your skeleton into 15 to 20 pieces of various sizes. The more pieces you create, the harder it will be to find them later. Write down the exact number of bone pieces you created.

Fill a shoebox with about an inch of potting soil or dirt (approximately 6 cups). Scatter the pieces of your skeleton inside the box. Push some bones down under the soil and leave some closer to the top. Add another inch (about 6 more cups) of dirt or soil to the shoebox to evenly cover all the bones.

Extra Credit

Create a more realistic skeleton by sculpting at least 15 animal bones from air-dry modeling clay. Once the bones are dry, scatter them into your archaeological site and see how quickly you can dig them up and piece the skeleton back together.

Now that you've created your archaeological site, use a spoon to scoop through the dirt and "excavate" the skeleton fragments. As you find pieces of bone, put each color into a separate pile. Once you've found each piece, try to piece your skeleton back together.

your body's attempt to warm itself up. Your body goes to this trouble because maintaining the right internal temperature is very important to an animal's survival.

Most birds and mammals (including humans) are **warm blooded**, which means their bodies can stay at a stable temperature even when the temperature outside changes. **Cold-blooded** animals such as reptiles and insects, on the other hand, cannot do this. These animals' body temperatures change along with the temperature of their environments.

Most animals have help managing their body temperatures thanks to feathers, fur, or body fat that slows escaping heat. A bird with feathers will fluff itself up on a chilly day, creating air pockets that hold in heat. Animals that live in cold **climates** often depend on coats of fur to keep their bodies warm. These animals may even put on some extra body fat to help them survive a long, cold winter. Marine mammals such as whales and seals have blubber—a layer of fat-like tissue beneath the skin. Blubber can be as thick as 12 inches in large animals like whales.

Along with the ability to regulate body temperature, animals' senses help them survive. Raptors such as eagles, hawks, and vultures are known for their keen eyesight. Andean condors and other raptor species soar thousands of feet in the air while searching for food way down on the ground.

Other animals rely on their sense of smell. The great white shark can smell a tiny drop of blood from miles away. Many fish can sense vibrations

and electrical impulses, along with small changes in water currents and pressure. Still other animals depend on a well-developed sense of hearing. Nocturnal animals that sleep during the day and become active at night, like many owl species, rely on their hearing and eyesight to track down **prey**.

Echolocation is a bonus sense found in animals such as bottlenose dolphins and horseshoe bats. To echolocate, animals make a sound, then listen for how long it takes for that sound to bounce off an object and return to them. By listening for echoes, animals can figure out how far they are from predators, prey, or obstacles. They can even determine how large an object is and whether it's moving or staying still. For animals that live in the ocean or in dark caves, this can be a crucial tool for survival.

Nocturnal animals, such as this screech owl, use their keen senses to hunt with little to no natural light.
Courtesy of Tampa's Lowry Park Zoo / Dave Parkinson

Play the Dolphin Echolocation Game

Dolphins must be able to navigate underwater, even when it's dark or murky. To do this, they rely on echolocation instead of eyesight. Pretend you're a dolphin using its extra-special sense—echolocation—to find fish. This activity requires a large, open space and a group of at least three people.

MATERIALS

🐦 Blindfold

Choose two players—one to be the dolphin and one to be the fish. All the rest of the players will be seaweed. As a group, define the area of play by setting up boundaries that no one will be able to pass.

Have the dolphin stand in the middle of the space. Blindfold the dolphin so he or she can't see anything. The dolphin will need to rely on his or her hearing to find and capture the fish.

The remaining players should spread out around the space. The fish will be able to move, but the seaweed should choose a spot and stay still.

The dolphin begins the game by saying "dolphin." Whenever the dolphin says "dolphin," the fish must say "fish" and the seaweed must say "seaweed," imitating the echo a dolphin would hear and interpret if it were echolocating in the wild.

If you're the dolphin, listen carefully to the echoes to find the fish among the seaweed. When you hear the fish, walk toward it and try to catch it. Say "dolphin" as many times as you'd like to make sure you don't lose the fish as it attempts to escape.

If you're the fish, you can move as much as you want, but you must always respond to the dolphin's call by saying "fish." You must also walk "heel toe," meaning you must take small steps by touching the heel of one foot to the toe of the other foot as you move forward.

Continue playing until the dolphin finds the fish and tags it. The fish then becomes the dolphin for the next round. Play until everyone has had a chance to be a dolphin and a fish.

Extra Credit

If you have four or more people in your group, try adding more than one fish to your ocean. To make the game more challenging, enforce a rule that says the dolphin is "out" if he or she runs into any seaweed.

Dazzling Defenders

Animals' unique forms sometimes function as built-in defenses that help them survive in the wild. The African crested porcupine, for instance, has a body full of barbed quills. When a predator is nearby, a porcupine sticks up its quills, kind of like the hair on your arms when you get goose bumps. While it wouldn't be wise to sneak up on a porcupine, the myth that says these spiky creatures can shoot their quills at attackers isn't true. Porcupine quills detach pretty easily, so a quill or two may fall off when a porcupine bustles up. But that doesn't mean it can aim and shoot!

Spines and scutes are two more built-in defenses within the animal kingdom. Some puffer fish species have spines covering their bodies that can help shoo away predators. When threatened, a puffer fish will suck in water to become big, round, and sharp.

Other dazzling defenders, such as the nine-banded armadillo, have tough, bony plates called scutes covering their bodies. These plates are like a coat of armor that helps protect an armadillo from becoming a snack.

Hoofed mammals such as white-tailed deer, moose, bison, and oryx have antlers or horns that help them defend their territory. During certain seasons, male bighorn sheep ram into each other with their tough, curled horns. These competitions often last for several hours until the weaker rival gives up and leaves. The winner earns territory and access to mates. Unlike deer species that shed their antlers every year and regrow them, species in the bovid family, like bighorn sheep and gazelles, have permanent horns.

(left) Antelopes like this gazelle have permanent horns.
Courtesy of Tampa's Lowry Park Zoo / Dave Parkinson

(right) Deer species like this moose shed their antlers each year.
Courtesy of Allison Barden / sandwichgirl

Large animals such as bighorn sheep may be the first to come to mind when you think of horns, but not all horned animals are big. Male rhinoceros beetles have front-facing horns that come in handy when charging rivals during fights for territory, just like bighorns.

Claws or talons can also be great defenses in nature. One impressive bird, the cassowary, kicks and slices at attackers with the two sharp talons attached to the cassowary's middle toes. A tiger's curved claws can be equally deadly as it swipes at rivals and prey. Like house cats, most big cat species can retract their claws when they are not in use.

Other defenses include beaks, stingers, and teeth. Male and female walruses have formidable teeth called tusks that can grow to be three feet long. While walruses usually use their tusks for boring holes in the ice and lugging their heavy bodies out of the water, males may also use them as a weapon to scare enemies away or to spar with other males.

Many animals defend themselves with harmful substances called toxins. Did you know there's a difference between venomous animals and poisonous animals? Venomous animals inject toxins through a bite or a sting. Some venomous animals include black widow spiders, rattlesnakes, scorpions, and stingrays. Poisonous animals, on the other hand, do not inject toxins; they secrete them. Poisonous animals, such as certain species of toads, newts, and salamanders, produce a toxic substance on their skin that can be deadly when touched or swallowed.

Camouflage is another way animals' forms function as a defense. Some animals, like zebras, are naturally camouflaged with designs or patterns. The black-and-white-striped pattern on a zebra's body is called disruptive coloration. When there is a group of zebras, their patterns make it more difficult for predators like lions to pick out one zebra from the rest of the group.

When an animal's coloring resembles its environment, it's called concealing coloration or background matching. Cuttlefish are masters of this type of camouflage. The **pigment**-filled cells in a cuttlefish's skin allow it to change color to match

Not all camouflage is the same. Zebras' striped pattern often confuses predators when the zebra herd scatters.

Courtesy of DC Wagner / Nyaminyami Photography, LLC

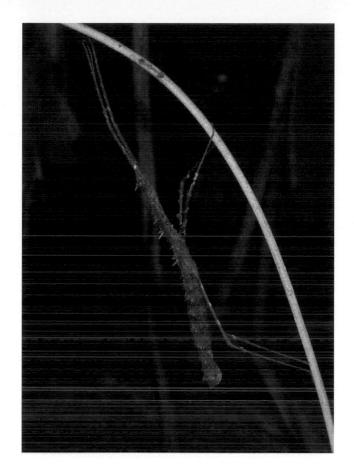

(above) Is that an eyelash leaf frog or a dead leaf?
Courtesy of Tampa's Lowry Park Zoo / Dave Parkinson

(left) Walking sticks don't wait for Halloween; they pretend to be sticks year-round so they can fool predators into thinking they're not food.
Courtesy of Daniela Schmieder

its surroundings. This helps it hide from predators and sneak up on prey.

Arctic foxes also benefit from concealing coloration. During the winter, an arctic fox grows a thick, white coat of fur that blends in with the snowy terrain. When the snow melts, the fox sheds its white coat for a brown-gray coat that matches the color of the ground.

Have you ever heard of an insect that looks so much like a stick that predators mistake it for something far less tasty than it actually is? These insects are called walking sticks, and they display a type of camouflage called disguise. The Solomon Island leaf frog uses disguise to look like a dead leaf on the forest floor. Thanks to its unique head shape, its dead-leaf coloring, and its dead-leaf texture, a predator might look right past a little leaf frog without even realizing it's missing out on something scrumptious.

Some creatures are copycats; they have camouflage that mimics another animal. For example, the nonvenomous milk snake looks just like the

Explore Concealing Coloration

In this activity, you'll be playing the part of a bird hunting for its next meal. Many insects in the wild rely on concealing coloration to blend in with their surroundings. How well do you think this tactic works? This activity requires a partner and a darkened room.

MATERIALS

🐦 Scissors or paper cutter

🐦 12-inch-by-12-inch sheet of brown cardstock

🐦 12-inch-by-12-inch sheet of green cardstock

🐦 Hole punch

🐦 Markers, crayons, or colored pencils

🐦 Flashlight

🐦 Timer or stopwatch

🐦 Tweezers

Cut two 1-inch-wide strips of cardstock—one strip from the brown sheet and one strip from the green sheet. Using the hole punch, punch 15 holes in each strip. Collect the brown and green punches. These will be your "insects." You should have 30 insects total—15 green and 15 brown. Discard or recycle the strips with the punch holes.

Next, use markers, crayons, or colored pencils to make your remaining squares of cardstock look more like a place an insect might live. For instance, the brown piece could represent tree bark—a place an insect may try to hide from predators such as birds. In this case, use a dark brown marker, crayon, or colored pencil to draw some lines that imitate bark. On the green piece of cardstock, you might draw in some blades of grass with a few brown patches.

You're nearly ready to play. Place the brown piece of cardstock in front of you. Have your partner set the flashlight somewhere in the room so it's pointing away from you. The room should be dark enough so that it's difficult, but not impossible, to see.

Once the room is dark except for the light from your flashlight, close your eyes. Have your partner scatter the 30 insects (both green and brown) on top of the brown cardstock. When your partner says "go," he or she will start the timer and you can open your eyes. You will have 30 seconds to use the tweezers to pick up as many insects as possible.

When 30 seconds have passed, your partner will say "stop." Turn on the light and count how many insects you've captured. How many green insects did you catch? How many brown insects?

Replay the game using the green cardstock instead of the brown. How many green insects did you catch this time around? How many brown insects? Switch roles with your partner to see how his or her results compare to yours.

> ## Tip
>
> *Think about what you've learned in this activity. When the green insects are in their green habitat, they are more difficult to find than when they are in the brown habitat. A predator will most likely go for the easiest meal available, so concealing coloration can be a powerful defense.*

venomous coral snake. By copying a coral snake's coloring, the milk snake appears to be more dangerous than it actually is. As a result, it's less likely to be eaten. Well played, milk snake.

Animals have some things in common, like their cells and the ability to move, but they really do come in all shapes and sizes. Whether it has gills to breathe underwater, a layer of blubber to keep warm, scutes that act as armor, or some tricky coloration, each animal must make the most of its unique characteristics to survive. In many cases, an animal must also adopt certain behaviors to take advantage of its special form.

Communicating with Color

It's common to think that chameleons change colors to hide from predators by blending into the background. While this may be partly true, defense is just one reason chameleons switch shades.

So why else do chameleons change colors? Most scientists believe the main reason is to reflect their moods. Like humans who use body language to express how they're feeling, chameleons communicate with other chameleons by changing colors. For example, if a male chameleon displays bright colors with red spots, he may be looking for a mate. If a female likes what she sees, she may change color to let him know.

Chameleons may also change colors based on the temperature and the time of day. A chameleon looking to warm itself by basking in the sun may change to a darker color so it can absorb more heat.

Similar to the cuttlefish, a chameleon can switch shades because it has special skin cells that are filled with different colors of pigment. While there is still much to uncover about chameleons, including exactly how and why their colors change, this survival tool certainly comes in handy.

Chameleons change color to reflect their moods.
Courtesy of Durrell Wildlife Conservation Trust / Dan Lay

2

UNDERSTANDING ANIMAL BEHAVIOR

On the island of Madagascar, an aye-aye sits perched in a forest tree. It's nighttime, but the nocturnal primate is well suited to work in the dark. It has large oval eyes, oversized ears, sharp claws, and toes that can grab on to tree branches. After spending most of the day balled up in its tree nest, the aye-aye is well rested and ready for some grub. But first, it must find some.

Using its extra-long middle finger, the aye-aye begins to tap the tree. As it taps, it listens. Inside the tree's trunk, wood-boring insects have carved channels through the wood. The aye-aye uses the sound of its tapping to figure out whether there is a meal to be had inside this tree. Tonight it's in luck; the aye-aye likes what it hears. With its long, skinny finger, the aye-aye digs into the tree, scoops out the insects, and eats them.

The aye-aye's unique **foraging** technique is just one example of a cool animal behavior. Whether it's foraging, hunting, grooming, or looking for a mate, animal behavior includes anything and everything

This strange-looking animal from Madagascar is called an aye-aye.
Courtesy of Duke Lemur Center / David Haring

an animal does. The study of animal behavior helps zoologists understand all kinds of things, such as why some animals live in groups while others live alone. It has even shown us that some animals can learn and that most have special ways of communicating.

Zoologists often refer to animal behaviors as **innate**, learned, or complex. Animals are born with a basic set of survival knowledge and/or skills. This knowledge is innate, which means it is not taught or learned and it can be performed the first time without practice. When a baby bird reaches up to its parent's beak for food, the behavior is automatic and unlearned—in other words, it is innate.

Learned behaviors are those an animal develops as it gains life experience. Just like human toddlers who learn how to be human by watching their siblings, classmates, and parents, animals often learn by watching members of their own species and imitating the behaviors they see. In some cases, animals learn by practice. Lion cubs practice stalking and pouncing by roughhousing with their brothers and sisters. Later in life, lions use these skills to hunt or to defend their group.

Most animal behavior is complex—a combination of both innate and learned behaviors. Complex behaviors begin with an animal's instinct, which the animal then perfects through life experience. The aye-aye's foraging technique is most likely a complex behavior, as is a lion's stalking behavior. Zoologists do not understand exactly how and why animals develop their behaviors, but

(left) Aye-ayes use their extra-long middle fingers to tap tree trunks, find insects, and then scoop the insects out.
Courtesy of Duke Lemur Center / David Haring

(right) Baby birds reaching up to their parent's beak for food is one example of an innate behavior.
Courtesy of Tampa's Lowry Park Zoo / Dave Parkinson

these mysteries are part of what makes the field of zoology so exciting.

Animal Smarts

Animals may not need to take multiplication tests, but different forms of intelligence—such as the ability to learn, remember, and adapt—can be an advantage when living in the wild. Remember how important it is for an animal to regulate its body temperature? Just like humans who seek shade (or air-conditioned buildings) during the summer and wear warm coats during the winter, animals don't just rely on fur and blubber to keep warm; they often change their behavior to keep themselves as comfortable as possible.

The chuckwalla, a desert-dwelling lizard found in the southwestern United States and Mexico, has mastered this skill. In the early mornings, chuckwallas lie out on rocks and bask in the sun to raise their body temperatures. If a chuckwalla needs to cool down or avoid predators, it will seek a shady rock crevice. This simple strategy helps chuckwallas keep their bodies from freezing or overheating in their harsh desert habitat.

Some animals regulate their body temperatures during the long winter months by hibernating. **Hibernation** is a state of inactivity in which an animal's body temperature drops to just a few degrees above freezing.

How does this help? When it's cold, animals' bodies need to use more energy to stay warm. Energy requires food, which is often harder to

Young lions learn to stalk and pounce by watching the adults and goofing around with other cubs.
Courtesy of Mark Gonka

Chuckwallas take temperature control into their own hands. They bask in the early morning sunshine to warm their bodies, then find shade when they need to cool off.
Courtesy of Phoenix Zoo

find during the winter. When an animal such as the Arctic ground squirrel hibernates, it saves precious energy by slowing its heart rate, slowing its breathing rate, and allowing its body temperature to sink to extreme lows.

Winter sleep is a less intense version of hibernation. When an animal enters winter sleep, its heart rate slows, but its body temperature does not drop as low as it would during true hibernation. Brown bears like Kodiaks and grizzlies are known to find a snug den and enter winter sleep for several months during the cold parts of the year. Unlike true hibernators that awaken slowly, animals in winter sleep can be easily woken up if disturbed.

Some animals travel long distances to escape extreme temperatures. This journey, called **migration**, often follows the seasons. Caribou herds travel south for the winter and back north for the summer. Bird species such as the Canada goose also migrate to avoid the extreme heat or cold. By traveling to a place with a more comfortable climate, migratory birds have access to food and shelter year-round.

Emperor penguins huddle together to keep warm.
Courtesy of Allison Barden / sandwichgirl

Large marine mammals like humpback and gray whales also migrate long distances to find food such as krill, plankton, or shrimp. Gray whales can travel up to 12,500 miles each year, which would be like swimming from San Francisco, California, to Rome, Italy, and back again!

Some animals are known for their ability to problem solve. New Caledonian crows are one of relatively few species that can create tools using objects in their natural environment. These forest birds use vines, leaves, twigs, or whatever else is available to make hooks that can help them catch insects hiding in the folds of a tree's trunk.

Animals that can learn to use the resources in their natural environment in new ways may give themselves an advantage over those that do not. Scientists have observed the veined octopus collecting and carrying coconut shells that it later builds into a shelter. This type of resourcefulness suggests some forward thinking and inventiveness. Sea otters also use existing objects as tools. They seem to have figured out how to use rocks to break open the shellfish they catch for food.

Living and Growing

Like humans, many animals have social lives. Some animals' social behavior includes living in a group like a pride of lions, a gaggle of geese, a school of fish, a pod of whales, a colony of honeybees, or a herd of wildebeest.

Group living has its advantages. Laughing kookaburra bird families stick together to help raise their young. Emperor penguins huddle

Test Your Sense of Direction

Many animal species, such as homing pigeons, seem to have a built-in compass. For migratory animals, this innate sense of direction helps them get back home, even when they've traveled far away. While humans tend to use signposts and landmarks to navigate, nonhuman animals' sense of direction may be tied to Earth's magnetic field. Pretend to be a homing pigeon as you test your own built-in compass.

This activity requires a partner and a wide, open space such as a backyard, a field, or a park. A space with some varied vegetation and terrain works best.

Tip

Make this activity easier by drawing routes with fewer twists and turns. Make it more difficult by adding more twists and turns or by turning the homing pigeon in a few circles before leading him or her along your migratory route.

MATERIALS

- Pen or pencil
- Notebook
- Blindfold

Objective

Lead your blindfolded partner (the "homing pigeon") on an unpredictable path, then see if he or she can find the way home.

How to Play

Make a quick sketch of your playing space in a notebook. Mark two points on the sketch: a start point and a finish point. Choose places you'll be able to remember, such as a tree, a bush, a fence, or a rock on the ground. Make sure your partner doesn't see what you're sketching.

Draw a route between the two points on your map. The route can have as many twists and turns as you'd like.

Now that your map is complete, mark the finish point by drawing an X in the dirt or by sticking a tree branch in the ground. Your partner can watch you mark the finish point, but do not mark the start point; it's a secret!

Blindfold the homing pigeon and lead him or her to your secret start point. Take your partner's arm and slowly lead him or her along the twisty, turny route you've planned on your map. Once you arrive at the end point, remove your partner's blindfold.

If you're the homing pigeon, it's your turn. Try to find your way back to the secret start point by retracing the steps you took while blindfolded. If you're unsure, make your best guess.

Take a look at your partner's map and compare where you ended up with the true start point. Did you make it home? Switch roles and play again.

(*left*) Herd living makes it more difficult for predators to attack individuals.

Courtesy of Mark Gonka

(*right*) Schools of fish swim in packs, coordinating their movements so they appear to move as one massive blob.

© *Shedd Aquarium / Brenna Hernandez*

together to keep each other warm in the frigid Antarctic climate. Termites also live in groups. Termite colonies are highly structured; each group member has a specific job that helps everyone else.

Many animals that live together depend on each other to survive. African wild dogs hunt in packs, allowing them to bring down antelopes and other large prey. Unique among birds, Harris's hawks also hunt in groups. The hawks take turns swooping down and chasing their prey until it's worn out and vulnerable. That is when the hawks strike to kill.

In the ocean, group living can be extreme. Many fish species form "schools" in which thousands of individuals pack tightly together and coordinate their movements so they appear to move as one massive blob. Schooling is a social strategy because it helps group members find food and mates, but it is also a defensive strategy. Like herds

of wildebeest and other land animals, schools of fish protect each other by confusing predators and making it more difficult to attack.

When a group of the same species lives in the same space, it's not always harmonious. Competition for food, territory, and mates can lead to conflict, particularly among males. Fights for social dominance are usually just for show, although in rare cases, two animals may fight to the death. Territory is very important to some species, such as the hippopotamus. A male hippo will fiercely defend its group and its river territory against intruders.

Some animals prefer to avoid group living altogether, demonstrating solitary behavior. Red pandas live alone high up in the trees in the Himalayas of eastern Asia. After pairing up briefly for mating season, red panda mothers will spend about a year with their babies before sending them off on their own. Many other species also prefer solitude, including the Sumatran rhino, the mud dauber wasp, and the giant Pacific octopus. Solitary animals usually seek company only when it's time to mate.

Mating and parenting behaviors are important parts of an animal's life, but these experiences change depending on whether an animal is a male or a female. Females are usually the ones that lay eggs or give birth to young. But even among the females of the animal kingdom there are many different versions of what it's like to be a mom. For instance, human moms are pregnant for about nine months before giving birth. White-footed mice, on the other hand, are pregnant for less than one month. And believe it or not, elephant moms are pregnant for nearly two years! Unlike most animals, the male seahorse—not the female—carries eggs in his pouch until they are ready to hatch.

Putting Others First

Do animals perform selfless acts? In zoology, **altruism** is when an animal behaves in a way that helps another animal, even if it harms itself in the process. In some cases, altruism even means risking one's own life to benefit another. Some humans practice altruism every day. Imagine a volunteer firefighter putting another person's life before his or her own by helping a stranger escape from a burning building. Among nonhuman animals, altruism is rare and difficult to study. However, many scientists believe altruism exists in some form among certain nonhuman species.

Common vampire bats, which are native to parts of Mexico, Central America, and South America, share food with group members when they're unable to find their own. On the surface, this system of food sharing seems selfless. Take a closer look, though, and there is more going on than meets the eye.

Common vampire bats are one of just three bat species that drink blood, and they need to drink just about every day to survive. These bats live in small, tight-knit groups of mostly females. It seems a bat will regurgitate blood and share its last meal with another bat only when there is a history of sharing. If one member of the group tries to score free food too often, that bat is quickly discovered and cut off from the sharing system in the future. This type of altruism is similar to the phrase "If you scratch my back, I'll scratch yours."

The naked mole rat may also demonstrate altruism. These social rodents live underground in arid regions of Africa. Leading each colony of 25 to 300 members is a queen and her kings—usually one to three males that mate with the queen so she can reproduce. The rest of the colony has one main goal: to take care of the royal family. Sometimes this simply means digging for food. Other times, it means sacrificing themselves to protect the rest of the colony from intruders. While this behavior appears selfless, there may be an underlying explanation. Because naked mole rat colonies live in isolation, each mole rat in a colony is related in some way or another. They're all part of one big family. In this example, the naked mole rats seem to believe "whatever is good for the group is good for me"—even if that means paying the ultimate price.

Within the animal kingdom, there is no one way to raise a family. Parenting duties depend on how developed babies are at birth. Human babies, for instance, are not at all prepared to survive on their own. Therefore, human mothers and fathers must tend to their child for years. Many other mammals do the same. When koalas are born, they are blind and helpless. Koala mothers have a pouch, similar to a kangaroo's pouch, where their babies, or "joeys," live for about six months after birth.

Hands-on parenting is not limited to mammals. There are some groups of fish, such as mouthbrooding cichlids, that shelter hatchlings inside their mouths and throats until their young can escape predators on their own.

For many species, though, parenting behaviors are few and far between. After mating and reproducing, many animals leave their young to survive, grow, and develop into adults on their own. For insects and amphibians that undergo **metamorphosis**, the development from birth to adult requires some major changes.

Without a mother or father around to help, the first part of an animal's life can be perilous. Green sea turtle mothers are quite famous for burying their eggs on a sandy beach and leaving their hatchlings to fend for themselves after birth. Because of predators such as gulls and crabs, only a fraction of young green sea turtles survive the trek from their nest to the open sea.

Speaking My Language

Communication is another important part of animal behavior, and this is true whether an animal is living in a group or on its own. But how can non-human animals communicate if they can't talk to each other? A good deal of communication can happen without words.

Try closing your eyes and imagining someone who is happy or excited. Is that person smiling? Smiling is just one way humans communicate that they are feeling happy. While in rare cases, animals like primates can communicate using facial expressions, body language is a more common method of communication throughout the animal kingdom.

Body language is different for each species and in some cases, for each individual animal. Your pet

(*left*) Seahorses are unique in nature because males become pregnant, not females.
© *Shedd Aquarium / Brenna Hernandez*

(*right*) Koala mothers care for their young for many months after birth.
Courtesy of Tampa's Lowry Park Zoo / Dave Parkinson

Big Life Changes

Metamorphosis refers to a major change in an animal's form, function, and behavior after birth. When an animal such as a frog or a butterfly undergoes metamorphosis, its appearance and its behavior change drastically.

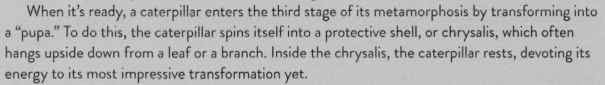

The four stages of a butterfly's life cycle: egg, larva/caterpillar, pupa, adult.
Courtesy of Jeffrey B. Vrieling

A butterfly's metamorphosis has four distinct stages, beginning with an egg. When an adult butterfly lays an egg on the underside of a leaf, the larva, or caterpillar, can begin eating as soon as it hatches. A caterpillar is the second stage of a butterfly's life cycle. Unlike adult butterflies, these wingless creatures have chewing mouthparts, which lets them eat and grow. In fact, caterpillars spend most of their time eating!

When it's ready, a caterpillar enters the third stage of its metamorphosis by transforming into a "pupa." To do this, the caterpillar spins itself into a protective shell, or chrysalis, which often hangs upside down from a leaf or a branch. Inside the chrysalis, the caterpillar rests, devoting its energy to its most impressive transformation yet.

The final phase of a butterfly's life cycle begins when it emerges from a chrysalis with newly formed wings. As an adult, the butterfly does not eat; it only drinks. During its short remaining life, the butterfly's behaviors revolve around mating and reproducing so the cycle can begin again and again.

dog, for instance, may wag its tail and perk up its ears to tell you it's excited to see you. Or it may tuck its tail and cower when it hears thunder, suggesting it's afraid. But this is not how all animals show excitement and fear.

In the wild, birds of paradise are particularly famous for their flashy body language. The Raggiana bird of paradise tries to attract mates through its dazzling feather displays and dances, such as clapping its wings and shaking its head.

Even if it's just for show, many animals communicate a warning to predators by trying to appear bigger, stronger, or more frightening. When threatened, polar bears and Kodiak bears stand up on their back legs to seem even taller than they already are.

Two polar bears stand on their back legs to appear as tall and intimidating as possible.
Courtesy of BJ Kirschhoffer / polarbearsinternational.org

Demonstrate a Butterfly's Life Cycle

A butterfly's metamorphosis includes four stages: egg, larva, pupa, and adult. Follow the steps below to demonstrate a butterfly's life cycle by constructing a metamorphosis wheel.

MATERIALS

- Pen or pencil
- 8-inch-diameter plate
- 2 sheets of 8½-inch-by-11-inch light-colored cardstock
- Scissors
- Ruler (optional)
- Markers, crayons, or colored pencils
- Paper fastener or metal brad

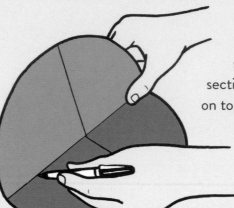

Fold the cardstock circles in half twice, the long way and the short way, so you have two intersecting folds that form a +. Draw lines on top of the folds, separating each circle into four equal sections. Use a ruler if you need help drawing a straight line.

Choose a cardstock circle and set the other one aside for later. Refer to the life-cycle illustrations on page 33. In the upper right-hand section, use markers, crayons, or colored pencils to draw the first stage of a butterfly's life cycle: egg. Label this drawing "Stage 1: Egg."

In the lower right-hand section, draw the second stage of a butterfly's life cycle: larva/caterpillar. Label this drawing "Stage 2: Larva."

In the lower left-hand section, draw the third stage of a butterfly's life cycle: pupa. Label this drawing "Stage 3: Pupa."

In the upper left-hand section, draw the fourth and final stage of a butterfly's life cycle: adult. Label this drawing "Stage 4: Adult."

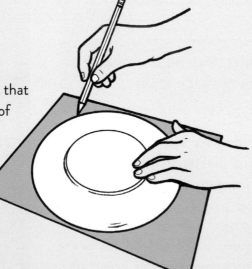

Draw a circle by tracing a plate that is facedown on top of a piece of cardstock. Repeat this step by tracing a second circle on a separate sheet of cardstock. Cut out both circles.

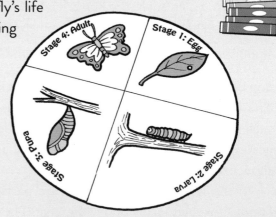

Stage 4: Adult

Stage 1: Egg

Stage 3: Pupa

Stage 2: Larva

Find your second cardstock circle, cut out one of the four sections, and write "Metamorphosis Wheel" somewhere on the front of the remaining ¾ circle. Place this circle on top of your other circle. Fasten the two circles together by sticking a paper fastener or a metal brad through the center of both pieces and bending the prongs back.

Arrange the top circle so "Stage 1: Egg" shows through the cutout. Turn the top circle clockwise to reveal stages two, three, and four. Demonstrate a butterfly's life cycle by showing off your metamorphosis wheel to a friend or family member.

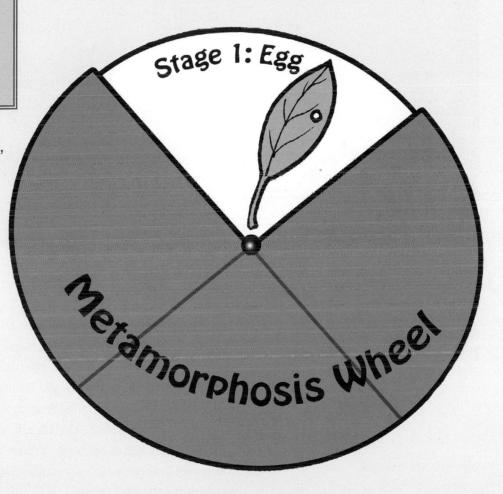

Nonhuman animals may not talk, but they have plenty of ways to communicate without using words.

Courtesy of Tampa's Lowry Park Zoo / Dave Parkinson

using sound. Whales are an extreme example of a species that communicates using sound. Unlike bird songs, which tend to sound musical to human ears, whale songs consist of deep moans, rumbles, and squeals. Blue whales and fin whales are known for their deep voices that can be heard from hundreds of miles away. Male humpback whales also "sing" to attract mates while warning rivals to keep their distance.

You have probably had experience with another animal that uses sound to communicate—crickets. A cricket's song sounds like loud chirps to the human ear. A close relative of the cricket, the katydid, also chirps by rubbing its wings together. Males use this chirping to call for potential mates.

Unlike body language and sound, an animal's lingering smell can communicate even when the animal is no longer there to deliver its message in person. Some animals, such as an ocelot, a wild cat at least double the size of a house cat, will mark their territory using urine and other scent markings. When a male ocelot sniffs another male ocelot's scent, it knows this territory belongs to someone else and it should stay away.

There are even some animals that use light to communicate. When organisms produce light without creating heat, it's called **bioluminescence**. Bioluminescent insects such as fireflies, click beetles, and a handful of millipede species have a special light-producing organ called a lantern.

Fireflies flash light in unique patterns to signal to each other and to attract mates. This type of communication is especially handy under the

The frilled lizard, found in Australia, also has special behaviors to say "stay back." Frilled lizards have folds of copper-colored skin that usually lie flat around their necks. When confronted, the lizard unfolds its extra skin, creating what looks like a big frill around its head. To make the effect even more dramatic, frilled lizards also rock back and forth, hiss, and bare their teeth to warn predators that they mean business. When animals show their teeth, there's a good chance they're trying to communicate a warning.

Nonhuman animals don't use words that we would recognize, but many of them communicate sea. In fact, most bioluminescent creatures live in underwater caves and in the deep ocean where sunlight can't reach. Aquatic creatures such as brittle stars, Leidy's comb jellies, flashlight fish, and anglerfish are just a few deep-sea animals that use light to attract mates, to startle predators, or to lure prey.

The deep sea may just be the most mysterious habitat on Earth, which means there is a lot we have yet to learn about how the animals that live there behave. Fortunately for future zoologists like you, the mysteries surrounding why animals do what they do are nearly endless.

By setting out to understand animals' forms, functions, and behaviors, you're well on your way to unlocking the secrets of zoology. And this is just the beginning. Get ready to take a step back and consider how animals interact with members of the same species, with members of other species, and with their environments. When zoologists study the big picture, it helps them understand what makes the animal kingdom tick.

Though some bioluminescent organisms live on land, most light-producing creatures live in the ocean, like this sea jelly.
Courtesy of Salah Baazizi

Communicate Like a Deep-Sea Animal

In the 1830s, Samuel Morse developed a code that helped humans communicate across long distances using beeps or flashes of light. This language, called Morse code, uses a signal for each letter of the alphabet that consists of dots and dashes.

Nonhuman animals use sound, body language, scent, and light to send messages to friends and foes alike. Pretend you are a bioluminescent creature living in the deep sea. Using a flashlight, send a secret message to a friend. This activity requires a partner and a darkened room.

MATERIALS

- Flashlight or laser pointer
- Pen or pencil and paper

Objective

Learn the rules of Morse code, then practice sending letters or a secret word to your partner.

Rules of the Game

In Morse code, a dot on the page translates to a quick flash of light. A dash on the page translates to a longer flash of light. The flash for a dash should be three times as long as the flash for a dot. For this game, plan to flash the light for one second when you see a dot and three seconds when you see a dash.

Take a look at the International Morse code key on the next page. To signal an A, you'd need to signal one dot followed by one dash. Practice signaling an A with a flashlight or laser pointer by holding the light on for one second, then turning it off, then turning it back on and holding it for three seconds, then turning it back off.

When you're signaling an entire word, you must pause between each individual letter. In Morse code, the rule is to pause for a length of time equal to one dash (in this case, three seconds) between letters. (Note: If you signal two of the same letters in a row—like the two Ts in the word *letter*—you pause for a length of time equal to one dot.)

Practice signaling each letter of the alphabet against a blank wall. Once you get the hang of it, write down a one-word secret message for your partner. Beneath each letter, write the Morse code signal for that letter. If you don't know where to start, try "SOS," which is a universal way to ask for help:

How to Play

After you and your partner have learned the rules of Morse code, bring your message and your flashlight into a semi-dark room. Have your partner bring a pen or pencil and paper.

Send your secret message by flashing the light signals on a blank wall. As you signal, have your partner write down the dots and dashes.

When you're done, have your partner try to decode your message using the International Morse code key. Did you successfully communicate? Switch roles and try a new word.

Tip

Make this activity simpler by taking turns signaling single letters on the wall. Make it more difficult by signaling a full sentence. The pause between two words is equal to seven dots.

INTERNATIONAL MORSE CODE KEY

A	• —		N	— •
B	— • • •		O	— — —
C	— • — •		P	• — — •
D	— • •		Q	— — • —
E	•		R	• — •
F	• • — •		S	• • •
G	— — •		T	—
H	• • • •		U	• • —
I	• •		V	• • • —
J	• — — —		W	• — —
K	— • —		X	— • • —
L	• — • •		Y	— • — —
M	— —		Z	— — • •

3

ANIMALS AND THEIR ENVIRONMENTS

Somewhere in the Sonoran Desert, a kangaroo rat munches on the fuzzy seeds of a creosote bush. A rattlesnake watches from its hideout at the foot of a saguaro cactus, preparing to ambush at the right moment. From above, a red-tailed hawk stands perched on the edge of a rocky cliff face, eyeing the showdown. What a delightful feast the rat or the snake would make, if the hawk could just avoid the rattler's deadly bite.

Nearby, a turkey vulture glides silently through the air, looking to scavenge on today's unluckiest victims.

The fresh carcass of a dead roadrunner catches the vulture's scent. It lands and gets to work, picking its meal clean before flying off, feeling satisfied. Desert **decomposers** like bacteria and fungi break down what's left of the roadrunner's body, returning it to the soil from which the creosote bushes and the cacti grow.

More than 10,000 miles away in a forest canopy on the island of Madagascar, a red-fronted brown lemur strips tree bark and munches on some juicy leaves. Despite keen vision and the ability to leap swiftly

A red-tailed hawk swoops down and snatches a rattlesnake.
Courtesy of Salah Baazizi

from tree to tree, the lemur has captured the attention of the island's top natural predator—a fossa. Stealthy and agile, this cat-like predator can not only climb trees, it can tread across branches like a tightrope walker.

Someday, even the fossa will die. Its body will become food for bacteria, fungi, and other organisms such as Madagascar hissing cockroaches, which recycle organic matter back to the earth, providing nutrients for the plants and the trees.

All around the globe, from the ocean floor to Earth's tallest mountain ranges, animals are interacting with one another as part of this cycle of life and death. Organisms are eating and being eaten; they are competing for resources like food, water, and space; and in some cases, they are helping each other survive.

Each living thing is part of a vast web of interconnected organisms. Remove a single organism from this web and it will create a ripple effect. Ecology is the study of this phenomenon, including how organisms interact with each other and with their environments.

Zoologists study ecology to help them understand how natural environments are changing, so they can work to preserve these environments through conservation. Learn more about how you can make a difference in chapter 6.

(*left*) Lemurs, like this red-fronted brown lemur, are an important part of the ecosystem in Madagascar.
Courtesy of Clémence Dirac

(*right*) The fossa is a cat-like predator related to the mongoose.
Courtesy of Clémence Dirac

Introduction to Ecology

Simply by being alive, animals are constantly interacting with their environments, including the air, water, and land. This is true for organisms both big and small. Humans interact with the environment by building houses and growing crops, by going for a swim in the ocean or a lake, and simply by breathing air. That means you are interacting with your environment at this very moment! Right now, wherever you are, you're taking up space, generating heat, and impacting your environment in dozens of other ways.

Living things are also constantly interacting with each other. Think of the different ways you interact with other humans on a daily basis. You interact with teachers and classmates, friends, and family members. The actions you take and the words you say often determine what the people around you do or say.

When humans help each other out, play games together, have conversations, and fall in love, they're interacting in a positive way. Unfortunately, human interaction is not always positive. Sometimes, humans interact in a negative way by hurting each other with words, actions, or weapons.

Among nonhuman animals, it's a similar story. Organisms affect each other in many ways, sometimes positive and sometimes negative. Ecology recognizes two different types of interaction: interaction among animals of the same species and interaction among animals of different species.

A **population** is a group of animals living in the same time and place that are part of the same species. You are part of a population of humans living in your hometown. Ecologists, scientists who focus on ecology, study populations in part by tracking population growths and declines.

Each individual animal within a population needs room to live, uses resources like food and water, and produces waste. All of these factors help determine how large a population can grow. When a population gets too big for its environment to support, some individual organisms will die or be forced to move because they don't have the resources they need to survive. It's all part of the balance of nature.

The second level of interaction ecologists study is among communities. A **community** is made up of animals that are part of different species. Consider the redwood forests of California and southern Oregon. Within these coastal forests, many different populations coexist together, including coast redwood and Douglas fir trees, as well as animals such as red tree voles (relatives of mice), barred and spotted owls, Roosevelt elk, and black bears. Each member of a community has a role, also called a niche.

Community Relationships

Sir Isaac Newton, a 17th-century scientist, said every action creates a reaction. Newton's idea applies to ecology in that each organism's actions—in fact, each organism's very presence—impacts its community and its environment.

Sometimes an organism's impact is obvious, like when a fossa hunts, kills, and eats a lemur on the island of Madagascar. This type of interaction is called **predation**. The fossa is a predator and the lemur is its prey.

Other times, an organism's impact is not as clear. When bacteria help fertilize the desert soil, it allows shrubs and bushes to grow, which provides food for animals such as kangaroo rats. As a result, bacteria indirectly impact the survival of kangaroo rats in the desert.

Besides predation, there are several other ways organisms interact within a community. In some cases, they compete. Members of a community may compete for space or for the same food sources. The goal is always survival.

In a lopsided relationship called **parasitism**, one organism benefits by harming another organism. A tick forms this type of relationship with a host, such as a deer. A tick latches on to a deer's skin, bites, and drinks its blood. In this parasitic relationship, the tick benefits by harming the deer. A mosquito that lands on your skin on a humid summer day is probably looking for this type of relationship with you!

Not all interactions within an ecosystem are harmful or negative. **Commensalism** is a relationship in which one organism benefits and the other isn't affected. When a pilot fish follows an oceanic whitetip shark around, eating the shark's meal scraps, the pilot fish gets free leftovers and the shark doesn't appear to be affected. Of course, it's difficult for humans to know for sure; there could be a benefit to the shark that we can't see or prove.

The relationship between cattle egrets and grazing animals may be another example of commensalism. When animals like cattle, rhinos, and waterbuck graze, they stir up the soil, causing worms and other insects to move closer to the surface. Cattle egrets are birds that feed on these worms and insects. The egrets benefit from this living arrangement because it's easier for them to find food. The grazers, on the other hand, seem to be neither harmed nor benefited by the egrets' presence.

Mutualism is a win-win scenario in which each organism in a relationship benefits. Like commensalism and altruism (remember the food-sharing vampire bats and the self-sacrificing naked mole rats?), mutualism can be tough to prove. However, there are some clear examples in nature.

You have witnessed mutualism if you've ever seen a hummingbird drink nectar from a flower. The hummingbird benefits from its interaction with the plant because it needs nectar for nourishment. The plant benefits from the interaction because when the hummingbird leaves, it takes bits of pollen grain with it. When an animal such as a bird, a bee, or a bat transfers pollen among plants, it can fertilize them, allowing the plants to produce more flowers. This process is called **pollination**. "Pollinators" or animals that pollinate are vitally important to their communities.

Ecosystems

An organism's community and the environment in which it lives form its ecosystem. The Great Barrier Reef off the coast of Australia is one of the largest and most diverse examples of an ecosystem on

Eat a Bat Fruit Salad

Fruit bats play a role in your ability to eat fruits from around the world, such as bananas, mangoes, and figs. Bats not only pollinate fruit trees but also spread their seeds—sometimes by sucking the juice from the fruit and spitting what's left onto the forest floor, including the seeds. These seeds can eventually grow into new trees that produce fruit of their own. By pollinating plants and dispersing seeds, bats help keep forests healthy and grocery stores full of delicious fruits.

ADULT SUPERVISION REQUIRED

INGREDIENTS

- Banana
- Mango
- Peach
- Dried dates (a handful)
- Fresh or dried figs (a handful)

UTENSILS

- Knife
- Cutting board
- Large plate or serving platter
- Forks and small plates for sharing

Serves 3 to 4

Begin by rinsing your selection of bat-pollinated fruits with tap water. Peel the banana and slice it into 1-inch chunks on top of a cutting board. Place the banana slices on a large plate or serving platter.

Slice the mango in half, starting slightly right or left of the center to avoid the seed in the middle. Ask an adult to watch and/or help. Set the smaller half aside. Take the larger half and slice off a 1-inch strip from the middle, which should contain the seed. Discard the piece of mango with the seed. Peel the skin away from each mango half, then slice the flesh into strips and place them on the serving platter.

Cut into the peach until you hit the seed in the middle. Slice in a circle so one half of the peach separates from the seed. Remove the seed and the tough parts that surround it. Cut the peach into slices and place the slices on the serving platter.

Add some dried dates and a handful of figs to your serving platter. Hand out some forks and serve some of each food item onto smaller plates. Explain the role that bats play in their ecosystems as pollinators and as seed dispersers to everyone who shares your snack.

Extra Credit

Bats help pollinate many other types of fruits and nuts, including papaya, agave, dragon fruit, guava, durian, cashews, and even cocoa beans, from which we get chocolate. Punch up your fruit platter by adding some of these tasty treats.

the planet. This vast network of coral reefs contains thousands of different species and their habitats.

Within each ecosystem on Earth, there is a flow of energy and nutrients from one organism to another. This flow of energy is called a **food chain**. When the sun beats down on a producer, such as a creosote bush in the Sonoran Desert, it fuels **photosynthesis**, which provides energy for the plant to live and grow. When a primary consumer, such as a kangaroo rat, eats the seeds of a creosote bush, it gains the energy it needs to live and reproduce. Primary consumers are herbi-vores—animals that only eat plants.

When a secondary consumer, such as a rattle-snake, eats a primary consumer, energy gets trans-ferred again. This time, the secondary consumer is the one that gains the energy it needs to live, hunt, and reproduce. Unlike primary consumers, secondary consumers are carnivores—animals that eat the flesh of other animals.

In some food chains, secondary consumers are eaten by a third level of consumers, such as a red-tailed hawk. In many ecosystems, there is an **apex predator** that sits at the top of the food chain, such as a lion in the African savanna.

Some species play an especially important role in their ecosystems. Sea otters are one example of a **keystone species** that has a far-reaching impact. When sea otters eat sea urchins, it prevents the sea urchin population from eating all the kelp—a type of sea grass that forms an important marine habitat for many different marine creatures. Sim-ply by eating their favorite meal, sea otters actu-ally keep their whole ecosystem in balance!

The cycle of energy within an ecosystem doesn't end with the apex predator. **Scavengers** such as turkey vultures feed on dead organisms, including apex predators. Worms, maggots, cock-roaches, bacteria, fungi, and other decompos-ers are nature's cleanup crew. Scavengers and decomposers play a key role in their ecosystems by consuming nonliving matter and recycling the nutrients back into the ground, which allows the cycle to begin again.

Earth's Neighborhoods

Some people in the United States prefer to live on the East Coast, while others prefer to live on the West Coast. Some prefer to live in the moun-tains, while others prefer the desert. Still others live in the South or the Midwest; each region has a

Sea otters play a crucial role in their environment.
Courtesy of Robin Riggs

unique set of characteristics that make it a good fit or a bad fit for a particular person or family.

Like humans, nonhuman animals have spread out all over Earth—from the hottest of hot places, to the coldest of cold places. Organisms have even found homes miles below the surface of the sea, where conditions are alien compared to what humans experience on land.

Unlike humans, other species don't decide where to live depending on where they can find a good job, where taxes are low, or where they can find the best pizza. Nonhuman animals live in the places where they are most likely to survive.

For a large number of species, the best place to live is in the warm, wet climate of a tropical rain forest. These lush forests support tall trees and a rich collection of animal and plant life. But not all animals can thrive in these conditions. In fact, tropical rain forests are just one example of a **biome**, a collection of ecosystems that share a similar climate.

Scientists have split Earth up into several biomes on land and at sea. In places called deciduous forests, trees drop their leaves during winter and there's rain scattered throughout the year. Deciduous forest biomes support a good deal of animal and plant life in the trees and on the forest floor. Taigas, or northern coniferous forests, are another type of biome. Taigas have long, cold winters and they're typically covered in cone-bearing trees like pines and firs.

Tropical grasslands such as the African savanna have high temperatures, little rainfall, and scattered trees and shrubs. Temperate grasslands, or prairie biomes, are dry and windy, often covered in grass, and are popular places for farmers to grow crops.

Desert biomes are dry places with sparse plant life and extreme hot or cold temperatures. The animals that call the desert home have special techniques to survive with very little water. Similar to deserts, tundra biomes are quite dry. These cold, harsh areas endure long winters and support few plants and animals.

The aquatic biome includes Earth's marine and freshwater regions. Marine ecosystems include the ocean, coral reefs, and areas called estuaries where freshwater sources meet the open ocean. Freshwater ecosystems include lakes, ponds, rivers, streams, and wetlands.

As you can see, each biome and the ecosystems within it support a unique combination of plants and animals. Each one is essential in preserving **biodiversity**, the diversity of life on Earth. Today, thanks in part to a new predator, Earth's biodiversity is at risk. Unlike natural predators, such as the fossa in Madagascar, this new predator has a tendency to disrupt ecosystems and damage the environment in which it lives.

Which animal has the power and the resources to sit atop every food chain on Planet Earth? You may have already guessed the answer—it's us, humans. Zoologists and other scientists all around the world must put their knowledge and love for the natural world to work to protect what they hold dear. As a budding zoologist, this is your chance to do the same.

The okapi, a relative of the giraffe, is native to the Ituri rain forest in central Africa.

Courtesy of Chicago Zoological Society / Jim Schulz

Construct a Food Chain

Zoologists study food chains to better understand each organism's role in its ecosystem. Learn more about the animals of the Antarctic as you construct a food chain that starts with a producer at the bottom and ends with an apex predator at the top. This activity requires access to the Internet or a library.

MATERIALS

- Pen or pencil
- 6 paper plates (substitute index cards if you don't want to decorate)
- Markers, crayons, or colored pencils (optional)
- Hole punch
- Scissors
- Yarn or string (less than a yard)
- Clothes hanger

Create one paper plate for each of the six organisms listed in the "Antarctic Food Chain" (right) by writing its name on the back of the plate. The organisms are listed in alphabetical order; your job will be to organize them into a food chain based on what eats what.

Antarctic Food Chain

Diatoms
Emperor penguin
Fish
Krill
Leopard seal
Orca

First, you'll need to understand each organism and how it gets its energy. Do some detective work by researching the six organisms. On the back of the plates, jot down what each organism eats and/or what eats it.

Begin organizing your food chain by identifying the producer in this group. Which organism gets its energy from the environment (particularly, the sun)? Write a number *1* next to the producer's name and set plate 1 aside.

Determine which organism is the primary consumer—an herbivore that eats the producer and nothing else. Write a number *2* next to that organism's name and set plate 2 on top of plate 1.

Next, ask yourself which consumer would eat the organism on plate 2 based on your research and label it number *3*. Then, which consumer would eat the organism on plate 3? Label it number *4*. Which consumer would eat the organism on plate 4? Label it number *5*. The remaining plate is this ecosystem's apex predator—the top of the Antarctic food chain. Label this organism number *6*.

Lay all six plates out vertically on your workspace, with plate 1 at the bottom and plate 6 at the top. Write the name of each organism on the front of the plate and decorate it by drawing a picture of the organism it represents. You may need to go back to your reference material to help you draw.

Punch a hole in the top and in the bottom of your six decorated plates. Cut six small pieces of yarn or string.

Extra Credit

Build more food chains by researching other Antarctic organisms such as squid, sea birds like albatross, and the blue whale. Hang these chains next to your original chain, then use yarn to turn it into a food web—a network of linked food chains. Connect each organism to all the other organisms that prey on it, even if they are part of a different chain.

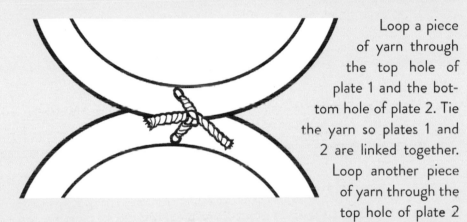

Loop a piece of yarn through the top hole of plate 1 and the bottom hole of plate 2. Tie the yarn so plates 1 and 2 are linked together. Loop another piece of yarn through the top hole of plate 2 and the bottom hole of plate 3, then tie it so plates 2 and 3 are linked together.

Continue linking the plates until you reach the top—plate 6. Loop the last piece of yarn through the top hole of plate 6 and tie it to the bottom edge of a clothes hanger. Can you see how a food chain shows the transfer of energy through the organisms in an ecosystem? What other ecosystems would you like to explore?

PART 2

Working on the Wild Side— Zoology in Real Life

"What you do makes a difference, and you have to decide what kind of difference you want to make."

—Jane Goodall, zoologist, conservationist, author

A muddy rhino.
Courtesy of DC Wagner / Nyaminyami Photography, LLC

4

ZOOKEEPERS, AQUARISTS, AND OTHER ZOO CREW

It's 7 AM at Nashville Zoo in Tennessee. As the early morning sunshine warms the ground, a gang of gregarious meerkats emerges from its burrow, preparing to bask in the first light of the day.

A few miles away, Bridget Caldwell, a Nashville Zoo primate keeper, is at home making coffee before heading to work. By 7:30 AM, Bridget will be preparing meals for the primates and other Nashville Zoo animals in her care. By 8 AM, it'll be time for Bridget to feed the meerkats and clean their exhibit—a place

for zoo and aquarium animals to eat, rest, and play by climbing, swimming, burrowing, or basking in the sun.

Before Bridget can take her lunch break, she and her coworkers will also tend to siamangs, red ruffed lemurs, African crested porcupines, and a red panda named Tsaka, in addition to washing dishes, doing laundry, and catching up on daily reports.

Bridget's work day may seem unique, but in reality, there are many thousands of zoologists who go to work each day at a zoo or aquarium.

A gang of meerkats hangs out.
Courtesy of Phoenix Zoo

It's up to the people who work in zoos and aquariums to come together in the interest of the animals in their care. In some cases, this means acting as the animals' guardians and caretakers by feeding them, cleaning up after them, and making sure they're happy. In other cases, this means overseeing other humans in various roles or helping to educate guests.

Each role within a zoo or aquarium is an important one. Because every single aspect of an animal's care adds to its quality of life, zookeepers, aquarists, and other zoo crew must be ready to accept the challenge each day on the job.

What Is a Zoo?

One of the best places to apply your knowledge about the animal kingdom is at a zoo or aquarium. A zoo—which is short for "zoological park" or "zoological garden"—is a place that houses wild animals, often from all around the world. An aquarium specializes in aquatic species like fish and marine mammals, though many aquariums also house some land animals such as reptiles and birds.

Zoos and aquariums provide places for humans to experience nature in ways that may not otherwise be available, especially for those who live near big cities. Besides offering places to have fun on weekends, zoos and aquariums help educate the public, support animal research, and contribute to conservation efforts. When you visit your local zoo or aquarium, you're helping these institutions fulfill all their roles—recreation, education, research, and conservation.

Zookeepers and Aquarists

Consider for a moment how you would feel if you had all the food in the world to eat but no roof over your head. You would never feel hungry, but you would be exposed to hot summers, cold winters, wind, rain, and snow. Without the ability to grow a coat of fur or a layer of blubber to protect you from the elements, your quality of life would suffer.

Now imagine how a kangaroo would feel if it had food and clean water but no room to hop around? Only when a keeper tends to *all* of an animal's needs can the animal be as happy and healthy as possible.

Zookeeping requires more than an appreciation for living things; it requires an understanding of zoology. By learning about an animal's form, function, behavior, and ecological role, keepers are better prepared to understand an animal and respond appropriately. For example, keepers must be able to tell the difference between an animal that is excited to see them and an animal that is showing aggressive behavior.

Unfortunately, keepers can't just sit down with an animal and chat. Animals communicate using body language, sounds, and scents, but not by using words. Zookeepers and aquarists must therefore find other ways to recognize and interpret an animal's needs so they can provide the best care.

When you want to get to know someone, how do you do it? In human society, spending time with a person is the best way to get to know

his or her personality. Similarly, zookeepers and aquarists must spend time with an animal if they hope to understand subtle changes in its mood or behavior.

Keepers must know each animal's individual history. They should find answers to questions like: Where did this animal live before it came here? What is its medical history? Has this animal been aggressive toward humans or other animals? Depending on the species, this information can determine how a keeper chooses to interact with an animal.

Zookeepers and aquarists must also study each species' natural history, including where and how it lives in its natural environment. A primate keeper should not only know about each gorilla she cares for, she should know about gorillas in general. For instance, since gorillas live in groups in the wild, they should live in groups at a zoo. Likewise, an aquarist should know that species such as clownfish and sea anemones coexist in the wild, so they can coexist in an aquarium.

A keeper's most important responsibilities fall into a category called **animal husbandry**. In the zoo and aquarium world, this refers to the process of caring for animals' physical health and mental well-being. If you are a pet owner, you're already familiar with animal husbandry.

Pretend you own a hamster named Peanut. As soon as you take Peanut home from the pet store, it is your job to make sure he has what he needs to survive. This means providing food, water, and a cozy place to call home. Whenever you clean Peanut's cage or let him roam around in a hamster ball, you're contributing to his well-being. In a way, you're already just like a zookeeper.

(*left*) Zookeepers and aquarists form special bonds with the animals in their care.
Courtesy of Mark Gonka

(*right*) Prepping animals' meals is an important part of the job for most zookeepers and aquarists.
Courtesy of Chicago Zoological Society / Jim Schulz

Zoo animals may not be house pets, but a keeper's core duties are similar to the chores you'd perform for Peanut, your pretend hamster. Each animal needs food, water, and a clean home—and this is true whether you're taking care of a hamster, a moray eel, or a Malayan tapir. But a keeper's job involves more than just the basics. Besides seeing to animals' primary needs, animal husbandry in a zoo or aquarium also means making sure an animal is as content as possible.

Enriching Animals' Lives

Have you ever wondered why pet stores sell bouncy balls, chewy bones, and fake fuzzy mice? It's because pets gets bored, just like people! Similar to pet owners, a big part of zookeepers' and aquarists' job is to make sure their animals are happy.

In the wild, animals must spend their time searching for food, water, and shelter. In a zoo or aquarium, humans provide food, water, and

AQUARIUM STAFF

John Rex Mitchell

Animal Programs Collection Manager
John G. Shedd Aquarium, Chicago, Illinois

"The awe and excitement on the faces of guests and staff when they get to see one of our animals up close not only greatly affects them, it leaves a lasting impression with me."

If you ask John Rex Mitchell, he'll tell you that visiting an aquarium can be just as diverse of an experience as visiting a zoo. John Rex works at Shedd Aquarium, where visitors can find not only aquatic creatures like sharks, rays, and sea jellies but also reptiles, primates, and birds. John Rex oversees the animal programs team, which focuses on educating visitors at the aquarium and out in the community. His most important responsibility is supervising the care of the animals in this collection by monitoring their living conditions, diets, and overall health.

When John Rex isn't scheduling staff and attending meetings, he enjoys interacting with animals such as iguanas, blue-tongued skinks, painted turtles, a red-tail boa constrictor, whitespotted bamboo sharks, and various amphibians, among many others. He particularly looks forward to training sessions and educational encounters with guests. Occasionally, he even goes on TV to talk about animals! John Rex loves his job not only because he works with some really fascinating species but also because he gets to educate the public about the creatures that inhabit Planet Earth.

John Rex Mitchell
© Shedd Aquarium / Brenna Hernandez

shelter for the animals. Therefore, keepers must find other ways to encourage natural behaviors and to discourage boredom. This often means adding something to an animal's environment that will be fun or that will make them think.

Keepers provide **enrichment** to maximize their animals' sense of well-being. Enrichment can be as simple as designing and decorating an exhibit so it feels as natural as possible to the animal. In a meerkat exhibit, this might mean providing a burrow similar to what wild meerkats build in the African plains.

Making changes in an animal's exhibit, such as adding different plants to an aquarium or providing a new spot for a bald eagle to perch, are other ways to enrich an animal's environment. Change gives animals the chance to explore and adapt to new surroundings.

Sensory enrichment appeals to an animal's senses. If a keeper tosses a beach ball to a dolphin to play catch, the dolphin gets to see and touch something out of the ordinary. Covering the floor of a Komodo dragon's exhibit with crunchy shredded paper is also sensory enrichment. The paper gives the Komodo something new to hear and feel as it walks around.

Food is another type of enrichment for zoo and aquarium animals. By hiding food around an animal's exhibit, keepers turn meals into a game. Instead of just walking up to a bowl and eating, the animal must forage for its dinner like it would in the wild.

Keepers may also work with animal nutritionists to come up with some special treats for the

Zoo Meals

Animal nutritionists carefully monitor the diet of each animal at a zoo or aquarium. To determine the menu, nutritionists look to what the species eats in the wild. Next, nutritionists calculate the number of calories each animal needs and pass this information to the keepers.

Zookeepers and aquarists are typically responsible for preparing animals' meals. They must follow an animal's diet guidelines carefully. Animals' base diets are often split up into two meals per day, but feeding schedules vary depending on the animal. To help make sure an animal's nutritional needs are being met, keepers often keep track of each animal's weight. If an animal starts gaining or losing weight, its diet might need to be adjusted.

New food items give animals the chance to be curious and to experience new tastes and smells. Keepers and animal nutritionists often work together to provide approved treats. Around Halloween, many zoos carve pumpkins and put them in exhibits to add some variety to the animals' day. Some animals will toss the pumpkins around; others will dig right in and eat them. Other treats might include ice for gray seals or cantaloupe for raccoons.

Pumpkin is a special Halloween treat for this tortoise.
Courtesy of Phoenix Zoo

iPad apps are a unique form of enrichment for orangutans.

© Orangutan Outreach "Apps for Apes" / Scott Engel

for humans, cognitive enrichment for zoo animals can be challenging and fun. Orangutan keepers at several zoos across the United States are teaming up with Orangutan Outreach to participate in the Apps for Apes program, which uses iPad tablet computers as a form of cognitive enrichment for these intelligent primates. Apps for Apes enriches orangutans' lives through games, painting and drawing apps, and even musical instruments the apes can play on the tablets' touchscreens.

Other forms of cognitive enrichment accomplish similar goals. Puzzle feeders encourage animals to figure out how to get food from a contraption. This presents a challenge and offers a reward in the form of a snack when the animal succeeds. Making sure animals feel rewarded for their efforts is an important part of enrichment in all its forms.

Animal Training

Zookeepers and aquarists are passionate about providing the best life possible for the animals in their care. One way they do this is by putting their animals in a training program. Animals that participate in consistent training routines tend to enjoy better-quality lives.

As a form of behavioral enrichment, animal training offers several benefits in a zoo or aquarium setting. It enhances the relationship between an animal and its keepers by adding a way for them to communicate. Keepers who work closely with their animals are better prepared to distinguish normal behavior from abnormal behavior.

animals. A squirrel monkey might get unsweetened Kool-Aid, raisins, or condensed milk in addition to its normal diet. Fun food treats can be a great way to make an animal's day more varied and fulfilling. Every diet change in a zoo or aquarium is closely monitored, which is why visitors should never share human treats with the animals.

Social enrichment involves changing up an animal's social circle. This could mean introducing an animal to a new member of the same species, or it could mean introducing an animal to a different species. If you're a zookeeper taking care of a horse, for instance, you might bring a few goats into the horse's enclosure to let them get to know each other. Forming new relationships and observing others can be an enriching experience for animals, just like it can be for humans.

Cognitive enrichment challenges an animal to think. Just like memory games and jigsaw puzzles

Create Behavioral Enrichment

One reason zoos and aquariums provide enrichment is to encourage animals to express normal behavior, such as foraging for food. In this activity, you will play the part of a Scarlet ibis keeper. Your mission is to create an enrichment device that will encourage the bird to forage for its food.

MATERIALS

- 🐦 Cardboard tube (such as an empty paper towel roll)
- 🐦 Scissors
- 🐦 1 cup of packed shredded newspaper
- 🐦 5 gummy worms (substitute rubber bands if desired)

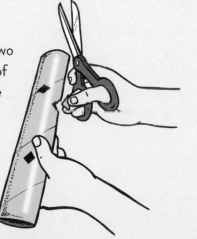

Flatten the cardboard tube and cut two triangle-shaped notches on one side of the tube. Avoid cutting notches in the inch at the top of the tube and the inch at the bottom of the tube. Keeping the tube flattened, flip it over and cut one more notch in the folded side.

Unflatten the tube. You should have three diamond-shaped holes. Roll the tube so one set of holes is

facing up and flatten it again. Cut three more triangle-shaped notches—two on one side of the tube and one on the opposite side.

Unflatten the tube again. You should now have six diamond-shaped holes. Close off the bottom of the tube by pressing the ends inward.

Spread the shredded newspaper in front of you. Mix a few gummy worms in with the paper. Fill the tube with the shredded newspaper/gummy-worm mixture. Close off the top of the tube by pressing the ends inward.

When placed in a Scarlet ibis's exhibit, the bird would need to stick its long beak through the diamond-shaped holes and search for a worm among the shredded newspaper. In real life, keepers would add real worms or grubs to a foraging feeder tube to entice a Scarlet ibis to search for its meal.

Extra Credit

Grab a pair of tweezers and try to forage some gummy worms out of the foraging feeder tube. Can you see how this enrichment device would encourage a Scarlet ibis's natural behavior?

A well-trained animal also has a better handle on what a keeper wants it to do. For instance, zoo animals frequently need to move from one place to another. Trained animals are less likely to feel anxious in these situations because they know what to expect.

One of the most important reasons to train a zoo or aquarium animal is so it can participate in its own health care. If a keeper needs to weigh a 6,192-pound white rhinoceros, he can't just pick it up and plop it on a scale. The rhino has to cooperate by stepping on the scale by itself. Lucky for rhino keepers, this behavior can be trained.

Similarly, if a pregnant animal learns to roll over and present its belly, a veterinarian will have a much easier time giving it a test called an ultrasound to check on the baby. When keepers train animals to participate in their own health care, it's much easier to help keep them healthy.

Training has its serious moments, but it can also be downright fun. Keepers try to make training sessions a rewarding experience for the animals. They do this by mixing up the routine, teaching new behaviors, and offering a variety of rewards. Training can be fun for visitors, too, while also supporting a zoo or aquarium's education efforts. Even silly behaviors, such as a walrus blowing a kiss to a crowd, can encourage visitors to appreciate an animal and want to learn more about it.

Before a keeper can train an animal at a zoo or aquarium, he or she must first get to know the animal, including what it likes and doesn't like. With this knowledge, an elephant keeper would know to reward an elephant with hay, not peanuts. The next step is to gain an animal's trust. Keepers establish trust through everyday interactions with an animal, such as mealtime. Animals feel good when they have a full stomach, so they quickly begin to associate those good feelings with the source of the food: its keeper. This type of positive interaction helps build a trusting relationship between keepers and animals.

Once keepers have formed a relationship with an animal, they can begin training. Keepers train using a method called **positive reinforcement**. When a keeper signals for an animal to perform a trained behavior and the animal follows through, the keeper reinforces the animal by giving it a reward. Can you guess the most common reward? If you guessed food, you're absolutely right.

Think of animal training like walking up a staircase. Each small step takes you closer to the goal. If you're walking up a staircase, the goal is to get to the top. If you're training an animal, the goal is to get the animal to perform a behavior when you ask it to do so.

With some patience and hard work, animals and humans can work together in some really cool ways. If you've seen an educational presentation at a zoo or aquarium, you know how impressive it can be to watch well-trained animals show off their behaviors for an audience. While most training has more serious purposes, like health care, keepers use training as a tool to add excitement and variety to an animal's day.

Making a Difference

Because zoos and aquariums are fun to visit, they can also be great places to learn. A common goal for the people who work in zoos and aquariums is to connect the community with the animal kingdom by encouraging respect and appreciation.

After all, visiting a zoo or aquarium is a much safer way to discover wild animals than trekking through the African savanna or diving to the depths of the Pacific Ocean.

Many zoos and aquariums give visitors the chance to learn through close-up or even hands-on experiences with animals. Some zoos have

Training Bailey

Pretend you're a keeper at a zoo or aquarium who is in charge of a sea lion named Bailey. You've already established a trusting relationship with Bailey by feeding her fish, her favorite meal, several times per day. Now, you'd like to take it a step further by training her first husbandry behavior—stepping on a scale so you can record her weight.

You must first find a way to tell Bailey "good job" when she's doing what you want her to do. Zookeepers use a technique called a bridge, often a whistle or a clicker, to signal to an animal that it's doing something right. You must teach Bailey what a bridge means (in this case, the bridge is the sound of a whistle). To do this, you blow into the whistle and immediately give Bailey her reward—a fish. When you repeat this process several times, Bailey will learn that whenever she hears your whistle, she gets a reward.

Another common training technique keepers use is called "targeting." Targeting teaches an animal to touch part of its body to a target object, such as a ball on the end of a pole. Before you can get Bailey to step onto a scale, she must learn to touch her nose to a target. To do this, you must have your target (the pole), your bridge (a whistle), and a reward (a bucket of fish). When you first hold the target out for Bailey, she won't have a clue what you're asking her

to do. To show her, you gently touch the target to her nose. As soon as the target touches her nose, you must reinforce her by blowing your whistle and giving her a fish. Bailey will begin to understand that whenever the target touches her nose, she'll hear a whistle and get a reward. Next time you show Bailey the target, she will most likely reach out and touch it by herself.

The last step is to get Bailey to walk toward the target, so you can eventually put the target over the scale. To do this, you slowly move the target away from her and wait for her to come touch her nose to it. When she does, blow your whistle and give her some fish to reinforce a job well done. Soon, you'll be able to present the target over the scale and Bailey will come right up to it and let you weigh her.

Coauthor Josh uses a targeting pole during a training session with Bailey.
Courtesy of Mark Gonka

Train Your Friends

Have you ever wondered what it's like to train an animal? You can use the same training techniques zookeepers and aquarists use with animals to train your friends. Give it a try! This activity requires a partner.

MATERIALS

- "Targeting pole" (spoon, stick, etc.)
- Treats (M&Ms, grapes, Cheerios, etc.)

Objective

Train your partner to do something silly using positive reinforcement. Your partner's job is to try to get as many treats as possible by figuring out what you're asking him or her to do.

How to Play

Begin by reading the "Training Bailey" section on page 61 to learn the basics of animal training. Have your partner choose an animal (and maybe even pretend to be that animal).

Next, select a "bridge." A bridge is a signal that tells the animal it has done something right. Examples of bridges are clapping your hands or saying the word "good." You can choose anything for your bridge, as long as it's consistent. In real life, you'd need to teach your animal that the bridge means "good job." In this case, assume your animal already understands.

Start by training a simple behavior such as a jump up and down. Lightly touch the target to the top of your animal's head, then give it a bridge (clap or say "good") and hand your animal a treat. Next, try to get your animal to jump by holding the target a little higher than its head. If it jumps, give the animal a bridge and a treat as a reward. If it doesn't jump, go back to the beginning. Touch the target to its head and give it a bridge and a treat, then try the jump again.

Once your animal jumps, hold the target a little higher. Then, a little higher. Be sure to give the animal a treat each time it succeeds. See how high or how far you can get your partner to jump for a treat.

Switch roles and try training a new behavior. Teach your partner to roll over, to follow you into the next room, or to flap her arms up and down like a bird. No matter what behavior you're training, be sure to tackle it one step at a time.

educational presentations or shows that allow visitors to see animals interact with keepers. Sometimes zoo and aquarium staff members help visitors pet a stingray, feed a giraffe, or get up close to a snake. These demonstrations are a great way for guests to learn about animals while also getting to know the people who care for them.

Programs such as summer camps for kids, volunteer programs for teens and adults, and animal-related classes for all ages are part of zoos' and aquariums' efforts to provide a fun and educational environment. Outreach programs extend this mission into the community. By sending staff members to libraries, schools, and other public places, zoos and aquariums can bring the experience to people who might not be able to visit on their own.

Focusing on education is just one way zoos and aquariums are different than they were in the past. Today, zoos and aquariums must obey laws by providing an environment where animals are free from thirst, hunger, malnutrition, pain, discomfort, fear, and disease. Animals must also be free to exhibit normal behaviors to the extent they wish to do so.

In modern times, there has been a major shift in the way zoos and aquariums design exhibits. Well-designed exhibits reflect an animal's natural habitat and act as a protective barrier between

(left) A zoo employee teaches kids about chuckwallas at an outreach event.
Courtesy of Phoenix Zoo

(right) Natural barriers keep zoo guests safe from the animals and the animals safe from zoo guests.
Courtesy of Chicago Zoological Society / Jim Schulz

> "If we can get people excited about animals, then by crikey, it makes it a heck of a lot easier to save them."
> —Steve Irwin, zoologist and TV show host, in a 2001 interview with Scientific American

Zoological Parks: Then and Now

The very first zoos and aquariums were "menageries," informal collections of animals, kept by ancient civilizations. The origins of modern zoos and aquariums can be traced most directly to the 1700s and 1800s, particularly in Europe.

London Zoo in the United Kingdom is one good example of how zoos and aquariums have changed through the years. For more than a century, British monarchs kept a collection of exotic animals in the Tower of London, a royal fortress with a long and bloody history. In 1831, after the Zoological Society of London was founded in 1826, the Tower of London collection moved to Regent's Park and helped form London Zoo.

For its first several years, the zoo was open to "scientific fellows" like Charles Darwin who wanted to come and study the animals in its collection. Darwin was a British naturalist who developed the theory of **evolution**. Members of the public could visit the zoo on Sundays if they had a note from a scientific fellow. As a result, many visitors came dressed in their Sunday best to see the animals. London Zoo opened its doors to the paying public in 1846.

Zoological parks began to open in the United States during the late 1800s. By the early 1900s, there were public zoos and aquariums all around the world. Many have enjoyed tremendous success and are still growing today, some welcoming several million guests every year.

Zoos and aquariums have come a long way from their roots as ancient menageries, but there's still work to do. By setting standards for things like veterinary care, safety, and expert staffing, organizations like the World Association of Zoos and Aquariums (WAZA) and the Association of Zoos and Aquariums (AZA) help make sure zoos and aquariums are moving forward, not backward.

animals and visitors. As zoologists learn more about the space requirements and living preferences of different species, they can continue to improve exhibits within zoos and aquariums.

Getting a Job

Animal husbandry—including enrichment and training—is a keeper's top responsibility. If you think you're up to the task, here are some points to keep in mind. The best keepers have good communication skills and are willing to be flexible based on the needs of their animals. They must be able to work as a team and to make decisions quickly, especially during a training session.

Keepers must also be patient and willing to work hard every single day. The job often requires dirty work, such as preparing food for the animals and cleaning up after them. For example, marine mammal keepers must cut up fish until they have the exact amount of calories needed for each animal. They might also need to scuba dive into a big exhibit and scrub algae off the walls. Other responsibilities include filling out daily reports and training logs and attending meetings with other staff members.

To get a job as a zookeeper or aquarist, you must typically earn a college degree in zoology or a related field such as biology or psychology. Each keeper's path is different, so don't be discouraged if your favorite college or university doesn't offer a zoology program. Many schools offer zoology-related classes in animal behavior, zoo management, or wildlife conservation. There are even

Plan and Draw an Exhibit

An animal's exhibit can contribute to its well-being while also providing a way for visitors to observe the animal from afar. Pretend you are in charge of planning an exhibit for your favorite animal at a zoo or aquarium. Try to balance your animal's needs with the visitors' needs. This activity requires access to the Internet or a library.

MATERIALS

- Pen or pencil and paper
- White poster board or sheet of paper (any size)
- Ruler
- Markers, crayons, colored pencils, or paint

Choose an animal for which you'd like to design an exhibit. Research your animal online or at a library. If you decide to research online, a good place to start is www.nationalgeographic.com/animals.

Write down as much as you can about your animal. Answer the following questions: Where does this animal live in the wild? What is the climate like in its natural habitat? What does this animal need to survive? How does it spend its day? What else is interesting or unique about how this animal lives in the wild?

Use the knowledge you've gained to begin planning an exhibit. On a poster board or piece of paper, draw a floor made of grass, dirt, or whatever material you'd find on the ground in your animal's natural habitat. Add some "furniture" such as rocks, plants, and trees. This could also include hollowed-out logs, a pond, or a small cave. If you'd like, label these items on your drawing.

Before you move on, make sure you've created an exhibit that meets your animal's needs. Does your animal need shade? If so, give it some tall trees or a cliff with an overhang. Should you include a heat pad, heat lamp, or heated rock for the winter months? Does your animal need a fresh water source such as a waterfall or a stream?

Decide how the exhibit will separate your animal from zoo visitors. You can use a fence with metal mesh, thick glass, or natural barriers such as a ditch or a moat. If you choose a ditch or a moat, indicate where it will go on your drawing. If you decide on a fence or glass, draw it in using a ruler and label it "fence" or "viewing glass."

If you are designing an aquatic habitat, be sure to include an area where visitors can look through the glass into the exhibit. Label this area "underwater viewing." Once you feel confident in your design, decorate it by coloring or painting the landscape.

Extra Credit

Take your design up a notch by adding some depth. Glue small rocks on your poster board to represent boulders, paint some cotton balls green to look like shrubs, or use blue construction paper to add a pool or a stream. Be creative with your materials to make your exhibit design look as real as possible.

schools known as "teaching zoos," such as Moorepark College in California, which focus on animal training and management. No matter where you decide to go to college, most degrees allow some wiggle room for students to specialize in their areas of interest.

It's important to supplement your education with some hands-on experience. In high school, look into volunteering at a zoo or aquarium, an animal shelter, or a wildlife rehabilitation center. In college, plan on completing an internship at a zoo or aquarium to gain real-world experience.

ZOOKEEPER

Steven Ok

Staff Biologist
Point Defiance Zoo & Aquarium, Tacoma, Washington

"As soon as you learn something interesting about an animal you like, find someone to share that information with. Not everyone takes the time to learn about the natural world. But you can inspire them with your enthusiasm, just like we do at the zoo!"

Steven Ok loves animals, but he also enjoys sharing what he loves about them with other people. At Point Defiance Zoo & Aquarium, Steven looks after some exciting species, including a Sumatran tiger, a Malayan tiger, a Malayan tapir, a lowland anoa, an Indian crested porcupine, an Asian small-clawed otter, a siamang, and a white-cheeked gibbon.

His day usually begins with a quick morning meeting with the rest of his team. Steven then helps check on all the animals in his department, prepare their diets, and clean their exhibits. At midday, one team member conducts a keeper talk for guests, while the rest of the team works on projects like fixing

exhibits, creating and providing enrichment, or recordkeeping. Before the end of the day, Steven prepares the animals' evening diets and evening enrichment, checks on them one more time, then securely locks everything up for the night.

Steven says one of the best parts of his job is getting to know the individual personalities of each animal in his care. While hand raising baby tigers, he'll never forget the joy of watching them develop from clumsy newborns into sneaky, mischievous cubs in just a few months.

Like other keepers, Steven's most important responsibility is maintaining animals' health. He also helps train the animals to participate in their own health care. As a leader of the zoo's enrichment committee, Steven helps create zoo-wide enrichment programs.

Steven Ok
Courtesy of Point Defiance Zoo & Aquarium

Because so many people want to be zookeepers or aquarists, you will face competition when looking for your first job. With an education, some experience, and a great work ethic, you can do it.

Being a keeper is just one of several jobs available at a zoo or aquarium. Some of them do not require a college degree. The grounds crew is responsible for keeping up a zoo's appearance. This means clearing the pathways for visitors, planting trees and other plants to keep the zoo or aquarium looking natural, and tending to buildings' maintenance needs. Without the grounds crew, zoos and aquariums would not only be less enjoyable places to visit, they wouldn't function properly. In fact, without the help of many departments—from guest services, admissions, and accounting to marketing, communications, and security—zoos and aquariums would not be able to achieve their goals as places of recreation, education, research, and conservation.

Other staff members dedicate their time to educating visitors about animals and their natural environments. Many zoos and aquariums have an entire education department whose job it is to coordinate outreaches and other educational opportunities for the community.

Volunteers also play a big role. Volunteers help support zoo and aquarium staff members in every department. Being a volunteer sometimes means standing near an exhibit and talking to visitors about the animals. Volunteering at a zoo or aquarium is a great way to share your passion for animals while gaining some experience in the field.

Like any other business, zoos and aquariums have managers. Curators, for instance, are responsible for the employees and the animals within their departments. A curator of birds would oversee all the animals in a zoo's bird collection. Curators typically make decisions about animal housing, training, and enrichment while also managing the keepers who tend the animals.

Veterinarians and their vet staff also play a vital role at zoos and aquariums. Veterinary medicine is a key real-world application of zoology that extends beyond zoos and aquariums to include pets, farm animals, and wildlife. In fact, while zoos and aquariums often seem front and center within the world of zoology, there are plenty of zoologists who work separate from these important institutions.

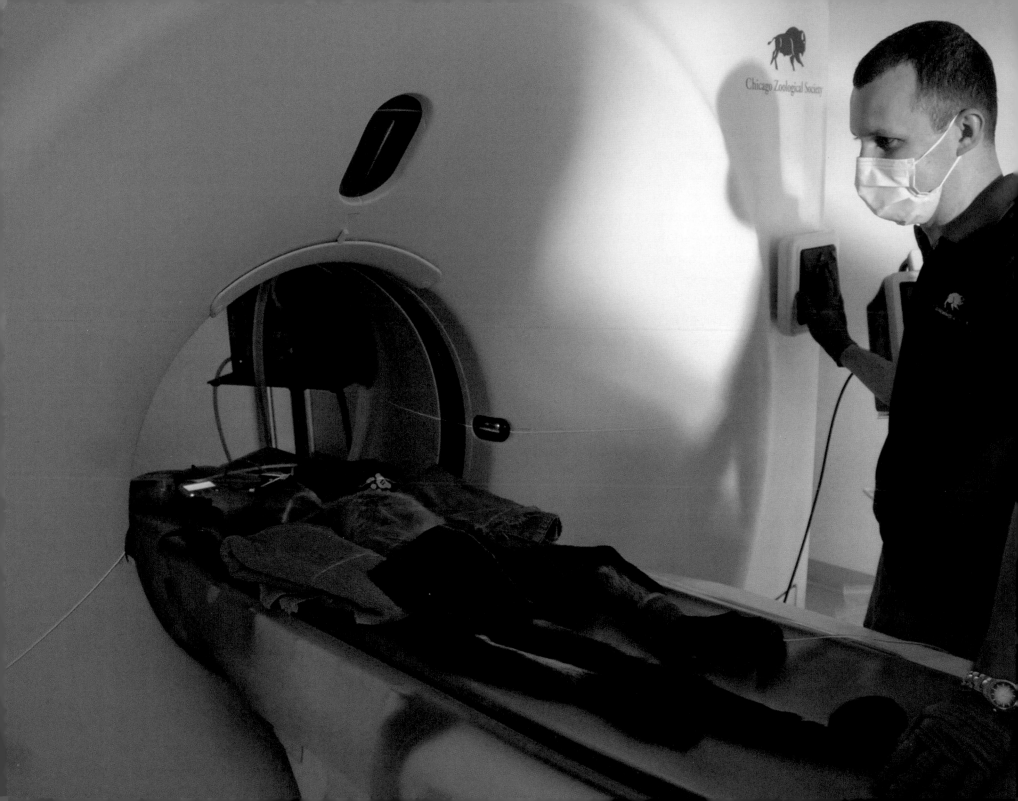

5

CALL THE DOCTOR! VETERINARIANS

For Dr. Mike Adkesson, there is no average day. As vice president of clinical medicine and one of several full-time vets at Brookfield Zoo near Chicago, Illinois, Dr. Mike oversees the health care of more than 2,500 animals—from tiny frogs, insects, and hummingbirds to rhinoceroses, dolphins, tigers, giraffe, and everything in between. Even after years of schooling and on-the-job experience, Dr. Mike's unusual patients challenge him to think creatively.

During one eventful day on the job, one of Dr. Mike's patients—a lion-tailed macaque recovering from leg surgery—kept removing the stitches from its wound. Dr. Mike was worried. If this wound didn't heal, the monkey's life could be in danger. Since Dr. Mike and his team couldn't sit the monkey down and explain that the stitches needed to stay, the vet staff needed to come up with a solution fast.

First, they tried to distract the monkey so it would forget about the stitches, but it was no use. The patient was too stubborn. Then, Dr. Mike had an idea; it was time for this monkey to put on some shorts. The team created a fiberglass cast that looked like a pair of

Injured animals must undergo medical tests before vets can diagnose and treat them.
Courtesy of Chicago Zoological Society / Jim Schulz

(*left*) This lion-tailed macaque, similar to the one whose life Dr. Mike saved when he came up with the "shorts cast," lives at Woodland Park Zoo in Seattle.
Courtesy of Woodland Park Zoo / Dennis Dow

(*right*) A veterinarian and a veterinary technician examine a small dog at an animal hospital.
Courtesy of AVMA

shorts—complete with a hole for the monkey's tail. The cast did the trick; it was too strong for the monkey to rip apart, so the stitches stayed in place and gave the wound time to heal. Even though Dr. Mike says this particular patient still gives him dirty looks, he feels confident that the innovative shorts cast saved the monkey's life.

The Wide World of Vets

Veterinarians must have a deep understanding of the forms, functions, and behaviors of a wide variety of animal species in order to do their job.

Vets rely on a foundation of biology and zoology to help them determine when a patient is healthy versus when it is ill. Detailed knowledge about an animal's body structure or anatomy comes into play every day. For instance, vets must know the differences and similarities between a frog and a toad, or between a dog and a cat, so they can accurately evaluate the health of these animals.

It is also important for vets to be able to anticipate how different animal species will react to a medical exam. Most likely, a vet would approach a nervous cat differently than a laid-back dog. Using their knowledge of animals' natural and individual histories, vets can make the best diagnosis and treatment decisions for their patients.

The number of species a veterinarian is responsible for depends on the type of vet he or she is. Most vets care for companion animals like dogs, cats, rabbits, birds, and other house pets. These vets often work for private practices or animal hospitals.

Some vets take care of farm animals such as horses, cows, sheep, goats, and pigs. Farm vets make house calls to perform checkups, to administer medicine, or to attend to a birth. Vets who specialize in farm animals may be employed by large farms or cattle ranches, or even as inspectors in the food industry. Animals that provide food for humans, such as cows and chickens, must meet certain standards of health, which veterinarians can help maintain.

Exotic-animal vets, including "zoo vets," treat many different types of patients, such as primates, birds of prey, marine mammals, insects, and pachyderms like elephants and hippos. Similarly, wildlife vets must be prepared to care for any wild animal that needs help—from deer, badgers, and opossums to owls, roadrunners, and snakes. Veterinarians who specialize in exotic species and wildlife often work for zoos and aquariums, animal sanctuaries and museums, or wildlife rehabilitation centers.

Veterinarians tend to have a working knowledge of many areas of veterinary medicine. Sometimes, though, vets bring in specialists to help them diagnose or treat a patient. Some vets extend their education by becoming experts in a particular species or category of medicine. For instance, an equine veterinarian specializes in caring for horses. There are also veterinary surgeons who specialize in performing complicated surgical procedures, veterinary cardiologists who have particular knowledge about heart-related illnesses, and veterinary oncologists who focus on treating cancer in animals. There are even veterinary ophthalmologists—animal eye doctors!

Dental checkups and cleanings are common during a veterinary exam. Many veterinarians can perform these basic services for their patients. For wild animals such as bears or tigers, though, even a simple dental exam may require **anesthesia**. Once "asleep," it is safe for a team of vets and their staff to check on and clean an animal's teeth. In some cases, a vet will bring in a veterinary dentist to perform more complicated dental procedures, such as a root canal or placing a tooth crown.

A vet checks a horse's eyes.
Courtesy of AVMA

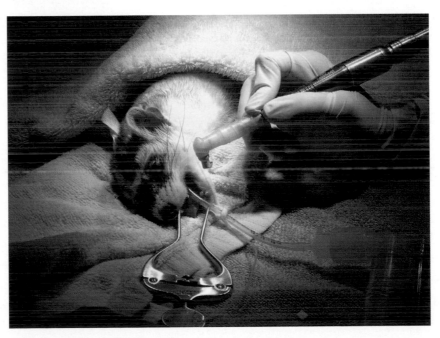

A ferret gets its teeth cleaned.
Courtesy of Phoenix Zoo

Mold Tiger Teeth

*Like human dentists, veterinary dentists need to know all about their patients'
teeth—from the smallest ferret to the largest elephant, and even ferocious
predators like the tiger. Pretend you are training to become a veterinary dentist
as you sculpt a mandible (lower jaw) and learn about tiger teeth.*

MATERIALS

- Plastic tablecloth or newspapers
- 2 pounds of white or gray air-dry modeling clay
- Plastic cup
- 4 acrylic paints or other craft paints (optional)
- Paintbrush (optional)

A tiger shows off its impressive teeth.
Courtesy of Chicago Zoological Society / Jim Schulz

Read "The Facts on Tiger Teeth," on the next page, before you get started.
Cover your workspace with a plastic tablecloth or newspapers.

Use the photos of a real tiger mandible from the side, front, and top
views (see the next page) to build a 3-D sculpture. Take two handfuls of
air-dry modeling clay and roll them out to create a V shape. This will form
the base of the jawbone. Shape the clay so the jawbone rises up in the
back; use the side view for reference.

To sculpt the 14 teeth that belong in a tiger's lower jaw, tear off two
large chunks of clay, six medium-sized chunks, and six small chunks. Sculpt
the large chunks into two pointy canines. The canines should be shaped
like cones that come to a point at the top. Sculpt the six small chunks into
incisors—the teeth between a tiger's canines.

Place the six incisors at the front of the jaw with one canine tooth on
either side.

To create the tiger's back teeth, form the six medium-sized chunks of
clay into cubes with pointy edges. Place three of these teeth on the left
side of the jaw behind the left canine. Place the other three on the right
side of the jaw behind the right canine.

Fill a plastic cup with water, dip your fingers in it, and smooth out the
clay using your wet fingers. Rub the clay where you placed each tooth
onto the jaw until the seams disappear.

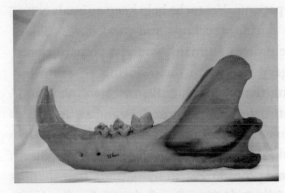

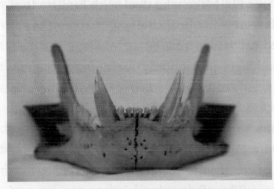

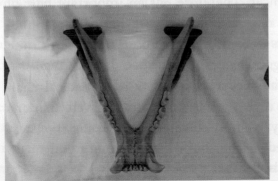

Set your jawbone somewhere safe and let it air dry. Then, if you'd like, paint each type of tooth a different color. Choose one color for the two canines, one color for the six incisors, one color for the four premolars, and one color for the two molars. The tooth closest to the back of the jaw on each side is a molar.

The Facts on Tiger Teeth

Tigers have 30 teeth total—a mix of canines, incisors, premolars, and molars in their upper and lower jawbones. A tiger's long teeth are called canines. Canines help tigers catch and kill their prey. Incisors are the small teeth located between the canines. Incisors are used for grooming and to remove finer tissues from the bones of prey. A tiger's back teeth consist of premolars and molars. These teeth have sharp edges so they can rip and tear through flesh.

A tiger's lower jawbone from the side, front, and top view.
Courtesy of C. Miguel Pinto

Vital Signs, Part 1: Build a Stethoscope

Veterinarians use a tool called a stethoscope to listen to a patient's heart and lungs during a checkup. Find out what it's like by creating a homemade stethoscope and listening to your own heartbeat.

MATERIALS

- 12 to 18 inches of plastic tubing, available at hardware stores (⁵⁄₁₆-inch width recommended)
- Small funnel (the tip of the funnel should fit snugly inside the plastic tubing)
- Duct tape
- Scissors
- Balloon

If needed, measure and cut the plastic tubing so it is 12 to 18 inches long. Stick the tip of the funnel into one end of the tube. It should fit snugly. If the funnel is too loose, use duct tape to secure it in place.

Cut off the open end of a balloon and throw it away. Stretch the remaining piece of balloon tight across the open end of the funnel.

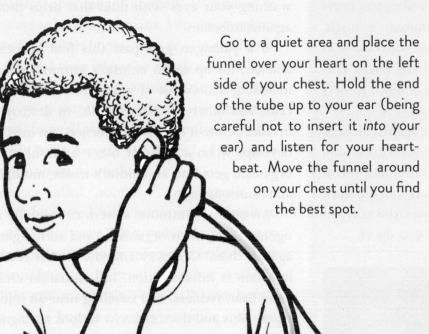

Go to a quiet area and place the funnel over your heart on the left side of your chest. Hold the end of the tube up to your ear (being careful not to insert it *into* your ear) and listen for your heartbeat. Move the funnel around on your chest until you find the best spot.

Dr. Mike listens to a wild dog's heartbeat.
Courtesy of Chicago Zoological Society / Jim Schulz

Vital Signs, Part 2: Take Your Vitals

During a checkup, veterinarians check their patients' vital signs, just like human doctors do. Find a partner and give it try. Complete this activity after building a stethoscope in "Vital Signs, Part 1: Build a Stethoscope."

MATERIALS

- Digital thermometer
- Chair
- Homemade stethoscope
- Stopwatch or timer
- Pen or pencil and paper
- Calculator (optional)

Begin by learning to take your temperature. Place a digital thermometer under your tongue and keep it there for about a minute. Take note of the result. A normal body temperature for a human is about 98.6 degrees Fahrenheit. Wash the end of the thermometer, have your partner take his or her own temperature, and compare results.

Next, practice taking your partner's heart rate. Go to a quiet space and have your partner sit in a chair. Place the funnel of your homemade stethoscope over the left side of your partner's chest and have your partner hold it in place. Place the other end of the tube near one of your ears (just not *in* your ear) and listen carefully. Adjust the stethoscope until you can hear your partner's heartbeat clearly.

> **Tip**
>
> *You do not need a stethoscope to measure your pulse. Place two fingers (your pointer and your middle finger) along the side of your throat, just under your chin, and feel around until you can detect your heartbeat. Count your pulse for 15 seconds and calculate your resting heart rate by multiplying the result by four.*

Using a stopwatch or timer, count the number of times your partner's heart beats for 15 seconds. Each *tha-thump* represents one beat. If it is easier, have your partner use the timer, telling you to start counting at zero seconds and to stop counting at 15 seconds.

Write down the number of heartbeats you counted, then multiply that number by four. The result will give you your partner's resting heart rate. If you counted 20 heartbeats, your partner's resting heart rate would be 80 beats per minute. The normal range for humans (aged 10 and up) is anywhere between 60 and 100 beats per minute.

Once you've calculated your partner's resting heart rate, switch roles and have your partner measure and calculate yours. Measure and calculate each person's heart rate at least twice. If you are measuring correctly, the results should be similar each time.

Getting a Job

Many young zoologists want to become veterinarians, so getting into vet school is competitive. A good overall strategy is to keep your grades up while you are in school. Veterinarians need to have strong math and science skills. Plan to take college courses in anatomy, biology, chemistry (the study of substances), and zoology.

Vets also need to show a passion for helping animals. Before applying to vet school, consider volunteering at a vet's office, an animal hospital, a wildlife rehabilitation center, a local animal shelter, or a zoo or aquarium to gain hands-on training. Future veterinary technicians and members of a vet's office staff should also look for ways to get experience working with animals.

In reality, there are many people besides vets that work in a veterinarian's office. Accountants keep track of money going out and coming in; office managers help run the business by managing employees, supplies, and equipment; and receptionists answer phone calls and schedule patients' appointments.

Veterinarians and all of their staff members must have excellent communication skills. A vet or vet tech must be able to communicate with animals' keepers or owners to catch problems early and to ensure proper day-to-day care. Vets also need strong leadership skills. They must be able to

> "Patient. Persevering. Caring. Compassionate. Dedicated. Highly-skilled and ingenious. These are just a few of the words that describe veterinarians, people who have basically given their lives over to the well-being of our animal friends."
> —Jack Hanna, zoologist and director emeritus of Columbus Zoo and Aquarium

make decisions that can sometimes mean life or death for an animal.

A vet's job can be a difficult one thanks to long hours, high-stress situations, and the inevitable loss of some patients. But along with this responsibility are great rewards. Keeping animals happy and healthy is a special privilege for vets, vet techs, and their entire team.

Part of being a veterinarian or any other type of zoologist is helping to better the zoology community. Some vets and vet staff donate their time to participate in research or conservation projects happening all around the world. Others volunteer for animal shelters or wildlife rehabilitation centers that take care of injured animals with nowhere else to go. By sharing their skills and knowledge with others in the zoology community, vets and their teams can make a big difference.

6

WILDLIFE RESEARCHERS

After a couple of stomach-churning hours in a local fisherman's boat, you've made it across the storm-roughened waters of the Sea of Cortez and arrived at your home base for the next 10 days: Bird Island. The late-morning temperature has already climbed above 100 degrees Fahrenheit. You stand on the rocky shoreline and wave good-bye to the fisherman as he jets off toward the mainland. As he disappears into the distance, you're surrounded by nothing but choppy waves. You wonder what you've gotten yourself into.

A quick survey of your surroundings tells you there's plenty of rock here but no trees or shade to hide from the sun. Good thing you brought a hat and sunscreen. If there's one thing this island does have, it's a generous amount of bird droppings. Suddenly, the nickname "Bird Island" makes a lot more sense.

Bird Island's real name is Isla San Jorge, a small government-protected habitat off the coast of Puerto Peñasco, Mexico. Here, you'll be spending some quality time with the salty sea, the blistering sun, and a colony of California sea lions. Your goal is to gather

Isla San Jorge is one of many places a wildlife researcher may visit to study animals like this California sea lion pup in the wild.

Authors' collection

(above) Isla San Jorge—
"Bird Island."
Authors' collection

(right) Researchers set up
camp on Isla San Jorge.
*Courtesy of Manuela
González-Suárez*

as much **data** as possible about the colony, their behavior, and their habitat.

You're part of a team of four researchers from all around the world. The group's first task is to select a campsite. You pop your tent on a flat space and help set up a makeshift kitchen in a small cave near the beach. For the most part, you'll be living off warm water, canned food, crackers, and granola bars until the fisherman comes back to collect you in 10 days. Since there's no reason to look forward to dinner, you look forward to beginning your work.

By day three of your research trip, you know the lay of the land. You've spent the better part of each day at one of two observation sites overlooking the California sea lion colony. You're a bit sunburned and sore but feeling good about the work your team has accomplished so far. You've taken a **census** of the colony, made detailed observations of the sea lions' behavior, and hiked around the island to collect sea lion poo. You'll bring these samples back to a lab to study the animals' diet.

At the end of another long day, you and your team members take snorkels down to the beach. You do your best to wash up, but the ocean water leaves you feeling salty. Tonight your group has some company; several sea lions are sharing the shallow water. You put on your snorkel and duck under the waves. A curious sea lion inches closer and closer until you're nearly face-to-face. You may be tired and dirty, but you're quickly reminded why you're here. It may not be luxury living, but hey, it's the life of a wildlife researcher.

Research and the Scientific Method

Zoologists who conduct research contribute to our knowledge about the animal kingdom, including how humans affect different species and their habitats. Research that tracks species' **breeding** patterns and their numbers in the wild helps guide conservation efforts.

A common goal in science is to explain what humans have observed in the natural world. Zoologists, similar to other scientists, follow the **scientific method** when searching for answers. This means they ask questions, brainstorm possible answers, test their ideas, and draw conclusions.

The first step in the scientific method is to be curious by making observations and asking questions. Susana Cárdenas-Alayza, director of the Punta San Juan project at the Center for Environmental Sustainability at Peru's Cayetano Heredia University, began her career as a research field assistant by asking this question: How do fur seals recover after a population collapse? She particularly wanted to know how fur seals along the coast of Peru were recovering after one of the strongest El Niño events in history.

El Niño refers to unusually warm ocean conditions along the west coast of North, Central, and South America. During the late 1990s, a particularly powerful El Niño event caused dangerous weather conditions in Peru and elsewhere. By collecting data about wild fur seals living along this coastline, Susana helped her fellow researchers figure out how El Niño continued to affect wildlife many years later.

Susana also serves as a field program coordinator for the Chicago Zoological Society, which supports wildlife research in Peru and around the globe. Today, she continues to try to understand the effects of the environment and human activities on populations of fur seals, sea lions, Humboldt penguins, and other species. She works with zoologists, biologists, and environmental scientists who want to find answers to their own questions about the wildlife living on Peru's coasts.

Researchers like Susana don't just ask questions, they brainstorm potential answers. The second step in the scientific method is to make an educated guess or **hypothesis**. If you played the "Explore Concealing Coloration" game in

Zoologists conduct research to answer scientific questions about wildlife.
Courtesy of Chicago Zoological Society / Susana Cárdenas-Alayza

chapter 1, you may already have experience coming up with a hypothesis. As you played, did you notice it was easier to gather green insects on the brown cardstock and brown insects on the green cardstock? If so, you may have hypothesized that in the wild, insects with camouflage are less likely to be eaten than insects without camouflage. Good hypotheses come from these types of observations and scientists' desire to know "how" or "why."

After coming up with a hypothesis, scientists design experiments that help them collect data by taking measurements, making more observations, or both. Testing and experimenting are crucial to the scientific method. If a question can't be tested with experiments or by gathering observations of the natural world, the scientific method can't answer it. This includes questions about philosophy or religion, such as "What is the meaning of life?"

The final step in the scientific method is to analyze the results of an experiment and, if possible, to draw a conclusion. When many different scientists test the same hypothesis and come to the same conclusion, the hypothesis becomes a scientific theory.

It's a Lab Life for Me

Experiments help researchers collect **evidence** that either supports or does not support a hypothesis. Some experiments are difficult to conduct in an animal's natural habitat because there are many factors beyond control that could change the outcome of a test. When this is the case, researchers might turn to the more controlled environment of a lab.

Lab research can help scientists learn about animal behavior, including animals' ability to learn, remember, adapt, and communicate. Labs that house live animals must follow rules that aim to keep the animals happy and healthy. Research labs that test human products on animals or that involve animals in medical research are controversial and beyond the scope of this book.

Some research labs are simply a place where zoologists can study data they've collected somewhere else. Researchers may observe animals at a zoo or aquarium, or in the wild, then bring these observations back to a lab. Once there, researchers enter data into computer programs that can analyze it, identify trends, and help researchers

Critical Thinking: Independent and Dependent Variables

To test a hypothesis, a scientist might set up an experiment that compares one group of test subjects with another group of test subjects. In the first group, called the experimental group, the scientist changes something to see whether it has an effect. In the other group, called the control group, the scientist doesn't change anything.

The experimental group and the control group must be exactly the same except for one factor—the independent variable. By changing just one factor, the scientist can see how this one factor changes things. The change a scientist is watching out for and measuring is called the dependent variable.

draw conclusions. Researchers share their conclusions by writing reports and articles for scientific journals and by preparing presentations for their fellow scientists.

Many universities have research laboratories. These labs allow students to study animals' forms, functions, and behaviors while they prepare for a career in zoology—possibly as a zookeeper or aquarist, a veterinarian, a wildlife researcher, or a conservationist.

The Laboratory of Medical Zoology at the University of Massachusetts helps the scientific community better understand infectious diseases that affect wildlife, including zoonotic diseases that can also affect humans. This particular lab focuses on studying tick-borne diseases, such as Lyme disease, in addition to human malaria and rabies. The researchers at the Laboratory of Medical Zoology help prevent the spread of these diseases by tracking outbreaks and by educating the public about the risks.

In the Field

A controlled experiment in a research lab is not always possible or preferable. Many wildlife researchers gather data to support their hypotheses through observation in the field. In zoology, "the field" does not refer to a random field full of wheat, grass, or flowers. Work in the field happens outside the office, lab, university, zoo, or aquarium. Field research often takes place in the natural habitat of the species being studied, such as Bird Island in the Sea of Cortez.

(left) Some experiments are best performed in a lab.
Courtesy of Stephen M. Rich, Laboratory of Medical Zoology

(right) A lab scientist works to collect and analyze data about zoonotic diseases.
Courtesy of Stephen M. Rich, Laboratory of Medical Zoology

Conduct an Experiment: Keeping Warm

It is important for any type of scientist, including zoologists, to know how to set up an experiment. In this activity, you will test a hypothesis that animals with insulation such as fur, feathers, and fat stay warmer than animals without insulation. This experiment will take 45 minutes to one hour to complete.

MATERIALS

- Water pitcher
- Measuring cup (with ounces marked)
- Permanent marker
- 3 aluminum cans (same size and shape)
- 3 quart-sized Ziploc bags
- Pen or pencil and paper
- 2 cups of shredded newspaper
- Spoon
- 2 cups of lard (available at grocery stores)
- Ice (enough to fill a sink)
- Digital food thermometer
- Stopwatch or timer

Fill a pitcher with 2¼ cups of tap water and let it sit out on the counter to reach room temperature. Use a permanent marker to label three aluminum cans and three quart-sized Ziploc bags *A*, *B*, and *C*. On a sheet of paper, create a table like the one in figure 1 to keep track of your data.

Measure out ¾ cup of tap water from the pitcher and pour it into can A. Can A is the control group; it represents the amount of heat an animal would lose if it sat in ice without fur, feathers, or fat to insulate it. Place can A in bag A and set it to the side.

Measure out ¾ cup of tap water from the pitcher and pour it into can B. Can B represents an animal that has fur or feathers. To represent fur or feathers, add a thin layer of shredded newspaper to the bottom of bag B and place can B inside the bag. Fill bag B with the rest of your shredded newspaper, making sure the can is surrounded on all sides except the top. Set bag B to the side.

Measure out ¾ cup of tap water from the pitcher and pour it into can C. Can C represents an animal that has fat or blubber for insulation. To represent fat or blubber, spoon some lard into bag C, creating a half-inch layer at the bottom, then place can C inside. Spoon the rest of the lard into the bag, squishing it around so the can is insulated on all sides except the top. Set bag C to the side.

Fill your kitchen sink with ice.

Take the "before temperature" of the water in can A by sticking a thermometer in the can and letting it sit until it gives you a steady reading. This could take one to two minutes, depending on the thermometer.

Record the before temperature of can A and seal bag A with the can and the thermometer inside. Place bag A upright in the sink so it's surrounded by ice. Start your stopwatch or set a timer for 10 minutes.

After two minutes, check the thermometer without opening the bag and write down the temperature of the water in can A in the row marked "Temp. 2 minutes." Two minutes later, record the water temperature in the row marked "Temp. 4 minutes." Continue checking and recording the temperature every two minutes until you reach 10.

After 10 minutes, check the thermometer and record the "after temperature" of the water in can A. Remove bag A from the ice and take the thermometer out.

You will now compare can A to cans B and C. Take and record the before temperature of the water in can B, then seal bag B with the can and the thermometer inside. Place bag B upright in the sink so it's surrounded by ice. Start your stopwatch or set a timer for 10 minutes.

At every two-minute interval, check the thermometer and write down the temperature of the water in can B. After 10 minutes, record the after temperature of the water in can B. Remove bag B from the ice and take the thermometer out.

Take and record the before temperature of the water in can C, then seal bag C with the can and the thermometer inside. Place bag C upright in the sink so it's surrounded by ice. Start your stopwatch or set a timer for 10 minutes.

At every two-minute interval, check the thermometer and write down the temperature of the water in can C. After 10 minutes, record the after temperature of the water in can C.

Subtract the after temperatures from the before temperatures and record the results in the row marked "Difference." Which can lost the most heat? Which can lost the least heat? Would an animal with insulation stay warmer than an animal without insulation?

FIGURE 1	Can A (Control)	Can B (Fur/Feathers)	Can C (Fat)
Before Temperature			
Temp. 2 minutes			
Temp. 4 minutes			
Temp. 6 minutes			
Temp. 8 minutes			
After Temperature			
Difference			

Extra Credit

Apply what you've learned about scientific experiments to answer the following questions: What is the independent variable in this experiment? What is the dependent variable?

WILDLIFE RESEARCHER

Dr. Manuela González-Suárez

Postdoctoral Researcher
Estación Biológica de Doñana, CSIC, Seville, Spain

"I am always looking for questions and answers. Although I am not out every day saving tigers or elephants directly, my work can help protect animal species, and that makes me happy."

If you think wildlife researchers are only either a) people with lab coats and microscopes or b) people with binoculars working in exotic locations, think again! According to Dr. Manuela González-Suárez, a biologist, zoologist, and researcher currently working in Spain, there are many researchers like her who wear normal clothes and work in a regular office—at least on most days.

Dr. Manuela has always had two key character traits of a zoologist: a curious mind and a love of nature. Looking back, she says becoming a researcher focusing on conservation biology was the perfect career choice for her. So far in her career, Dr. Manuela has done research work on spider behavior, lizard ecology, and mammalian conservation. Her goal is to be able to say her research has helped prevent a species' **extinction**.

On most days, Dr. Manuela rides her bike to an office where she has a desk and a computer. Her main job is to learn how and why species become extinct and then research what zoologists can do to prevent this loss. Though she has spent a good deal of time collecting information and observing animals in the wild, she's usually in her office analyzing data and writing about what she has learned.

As a wildlife researcher, Dr. Manuela must follow the scientific method. She thinks of interesting and exciting questions about nature, brainstorms hypotheses, designs ways to test her hypotheses, then shares what she learns with others. Because science is a continuous learning process, she says one question or experiment often leads to other questions and experiments. In other words, a researcher's job is never done.

A successful researcher must be able to work with others to get funding and support for projects. Researchers must also share their work by publishing in scientific journals, giving scientific talks, and, occasionally, participating in books like *Zoology for Kids*. Dr. Manuela says being a wildlife researcher requires dedication, but if you love what you do, all the hard work pays off.

Dr. Manuela González-Suárez, a wildlife researcher, helps gather data to bring back to a lab.
Courtesy of Manuela González-Suárez

Scientists performing observational research in the field usually have less control over their experiments. However, this does not mean observation isn't a good way to answer scientific questions. For instance, observation can help researchers gather information about how animals set up and defend their territories, how they find mates, and how they raise their offspring.

So how does a wildlife researcher perform research in the field? Pretend you are studying wild California sea lions on Isla San Jorge. Early in the day, you and a fellow researcher set up chairs and a shade umbrella on a rocky cliff overlooking one of the island's beaches, where hundreds of sea lions have come ashore. You bring binoculars, a pen and paper for taking notes, and maybe even a handheld electronic device for inputting data.

Your first task is to observe the habitat itself. You use grid paper to draw a basic map of the beach. You estimate the size of the habitat and make note of environmental factors such as air temperature, wind speed, and the position of the tide.

For the next few hours, you observe the sea lions by conducting 15-minute **focal samples**. To take a focal sample, you watch one sea lion closely and keep track of each behavior you see. After 15 minutes, you choose a new animal and begin again.

When wildlife researchers observe animal behaviors, they might use an **ethogram** to help them recognize and record behaviors quickly and accurately. If, during a focal sample, you noticed a male California sea lion making noise and circling its territory, you'd take a look at an ethogram like the one in figure 2 on the next page, recognize the

Zoologist Ramona Flatz briefly captures a wild California sea lion pup to gather some basic data.
Courtesy of Ramona Flatz

sea lion is "patrolling," and make a check mark next to the behavior on your worksheet.

Researchers also observe behavior using a technique called scanning. Scanning provides a quick sampling of an entire group's behaviors. Unlike a focal sample, which records the behaviors of one animal, a scan sample records the behaviors of a group of animals at one point in time. Scanning is like taking a mental snapshot of a moment and recording it for later.

Many field research projects require a census. A census helps researchers keep track of animals' numbers in the wild. As a wildlife researcher on Isla San Jorge, you'd need to take a boat ride around the island to count the number of sea lions that make up the colony. Most of the time, researchers are not only interested in how many animals are at a site, they also want to know the age and gender of each animal whenever possible.

"When I am exhausted from two days of travel, beat by sixteen hours of uninterrupted filming, or sick from an exotic bug that has set up camp in my lower intestine, I remind myself that I've got one of the neatest jobs in the world."
—Jeff Corwin, zoologist and TV show host

BEHAVIOR	APPLIES TO	DESCRIPTION
Patrolling	Males	Territorial male barking and circling territory.
Nursing	Females/Pups	Female nursing or pup/young adult feeding.
Female-pup calls	Females/Pups	Pup and female calling for each other.
Nuzzling	All	Animal sniffing at or passing its snout repeatedly over another animal's snout.
Scratching self	All	Grooming by scratching self against rocks, sand, or other animals.
Sitting	All	Animal resting on the ground or in the surf, front flippers are holding body up.
Resting	All	Animal is lying down; both sets of flippers are resting.
Locomotion	All	Animal is moving from one place to another.
Play	All	Pup/young adult simulating adult behavior.

Field researchers might briefly capture wild animals to tag them or to take samples. Tagging or marking animals for the purposes of wildlife research helps scientists keep track of animals more easily. This can be helpful during observational studies. Taking samples of an animal's hair, tissue, blood, or feces from the field to a lab may also be necessary, depending on the project.

After capturing a wild animal, researchers might also weigh it, take its measurements, and check its body for wounds. For small animals like sea lion pups, this is relatively easy to do without harming the animal or the researcher. For larger species, a veterinarian may need to step in to anesthetize an animal before it can be safely studied. Zoologists must constantly weigh the benefits and risks of interfering with wild animals for the purposes of research.

Research and Discovery

Discovery is an important part of some research teams' mission in the field. Every once in a while, a researcher will discover a new species while conducting a population census or observing wildlife.

The Monterey Bay Aquarium Research Institute announced in 2012 that a team of scientists had discovered a species called the harp sponge.

Backyard Zoology: Perform Field Research

You don't need to travel far to conduct field research. In fact, you can practice being a wildlife researcher in your own home or backyard, or in a nearby park, zoo, or aquarium, using the same techniques real zoologists use. This activity requires access to an animal you can observe for at least 15 minutes.

MATERIALS

- 🐦 Notebook
- 🐦 Pen or pencil
- 🐦 Timer or stopwatch
- 🐦 Binoculars (optional)
- 🐦 Magnifying glass (optional)

To conduct wildlife research at home, practice observing an animal and creating an ethogram based on your observations of its behaviors. First, choose an animal you'd like to observe. You can choose a pet like a cat, a dog, or a fish; a wild animal such as a snail or a worm; or an animal at a zoo or aquarium. We don't recommend choosing a wild bird unless you have a feeder that will tempt the bird to linger for about 15 minutes.

Set up your observation station with a notebook and a pen or pencil, a timer or stopwatch, and any other tools you may need. (If you're watching a zoo animal from far away, maybe bring binoculars. If you're watching an insect outside, consider bringing a magnifying glass.)

Set a timer for 15 minutes. Watch the animal you've chosen and take notes by writing down all the behaviors you observe. If you are observing a house cat, your list might include looking out a window, batting at a toy, drinking water, eating food, sleeping, stretching, grooming, playing, chewing on a cord, and going to the bathroom in the litter box.

If you don't observe more than two or three behaviors during the 15-minute observation period, try bumping your time up to 20 or 30 minutes.

When you're done observing, organize your notes into an ethogram that looks like figure 3. List each behavior you observed and write a brief description of it. Read through the behaviors and descriptions given in figure 2 if you need an example.

FIGURE 3: HOMEMADE ETHOGRAM TEMPLATE

BEHAVIOR	DESCRIPTION

Extra Credit

Try creating a second ethogram for a different species, then comparing how the two species spend their time. For instance, compare a dog and a cat at home, a squirrel and an insect outside, or a monkey and an alligator at a zoo.

(left) Wildlife researchers took this photo as they scanned a group of animals and recorded their behaviors, creating a snapshot of the moment that they could analyze later.

Authors' collection

(right) The olinguito, one of science's recently discovered species, is part of the same family as raccoons, coatis, and kinkajous.

Courtesy of C. Miguel Pinto

Thanks to the institute's remotely operated vehicles that can dive far below the depths of human divers, zoologists can now study this deep-sea sponge.

In 2013, a team of Smithsonian scientists revealed their discovery of the olinguito, a small carnivore native to the forests of Colombia and Ecuador. The team first realized the olinguito was unnamed and undescribed by the scientific community during a multiyear research study focused on a previously known species.

A wildlife researcher's goal is not only to gather information about known and unknown species but also to understand how each species fits into its ecosystem. Research, discovery, and documentation add to society's knowledge of the animal kingdom, which can be passed down from generation to generation.

Research can help zoos and aquariums take better care of their animals. For example, it could help a zookeeper or aquarist determine what form of enrichment an animal prefers. Or research could help a curator understand how an animal is using the space in its exhibit, which could help improve exhibit designs down the road.

Perhaps the most important function of wildlife research, though, is to drive conservation efforts. Research can help zoologists determine whether an animal is endangered in the wild and what can be done about it. It can help measure habitat loss and estimate what could happen if conditions do not change. Armed with this type of

Animal Classification

Zoologists have named more than one million species, but scientists believe this is just a fraction of those that inhabit Planet Earth. This means there is a vast number of species left to be discovered and studied.

Historians believe the Greek philosopher Aristotle was the first person to classify or arrange animal species into an order based on their similar forms. In the 1700s, a Swedish scientist named Carolus Linnaeus furthered this idea. Today, we classify each living thing by grouping it into a kingdom, a phylum, a class, an order, a family, a genus, and a species.

Carolus Linnaeus also developed a system for naming species called binomial nomenclature, which assigns each living thing a **scientific name** made up of two Latin words. Humans' scientific name is *Homo sapiens*.

CLASSIFYING A HUMAN, A GORILLA, AND A CLOWNFISH

	HUMAN	WESTERN GORILLA	ORANGE CLOWNFISH
Kingdom	Animalia	Animalia	Animalia
Phylum	Chordata	Chordata	Chordata
Class	Mammalia	Mammalia	Actinopterygii
Order	Primates	Primates	Perciformes
Family	Hominidae	Hominidae	Pomacentridae
Genus	*Homo*	*Gorilla*	*Amphiprion*
Species	*Homo sapiens*	*Gorilla gorilla*	*Amphiprion percula*

Invent a New Species

You're a wildlife researcher gathering data in a remote corner of the world. You come across a strange animal you've never seen before. Could it be an undiscovered species? Let your imagination run wild as you invent a species, draw it, describe it, and name it. This activity requires access to the Internet or a library.

MATERIALS

🐦 Pen or pencil

🐦 2 to 3 sheets of blank printer paper

🐦 Markers, crayons, or colored pencils

Do you love reptiles? Amphibians? Fish? Birds? Insects? Mammals? Think of an animal or two you'd like to use as inspiration for a brand-new species from your imagination. Begin with a rough sketch of what your species might look like. Look up pictures of existing species to help guide your design.

Once you've brainstormed your animal's basic form, consider where it will live. Give your animal some features that will help it survive. If you're designing a fish with 17 eyes that lives inside purple sea anemones, you might give it some bright purple camouflage to blend in with its environment. You might also give it a long tongue it can use to snatch prey.

Extra Credit

If you really had discovered a new species during a research trip, you would have written about the discovery in your field notebook. Create a pretend field notebook and make an entry about your discovery. How did the animal catch your attention? What behaviors did you observe?

Decide what your creature would eat, whether it would live alone or in a group, and how it would spend its days (or nights, if it's nocturnal).

Now that you've outlined your new species' form, function, and behavior, draw a final version on a fresh sheet of paper. Color your drawing with markers, crayons, or colored pencils.

Decide what to call your new species. If you'd like to name your animal "Jason's Regal Eye Fish," go for it! Write the name at the top of your drawing.

Last, make a few bullet points on your paper that describe your species' habitat, its diet, its survival techniques, and any special behaviors. Share your invention with a friend or family member.

data, zoologists who are passionate about wildlife can inspire others to step in and help protect the natural world.

Getting a Job

Wildlife research is a team effort. It takes managers like Susana who supervise projects, coordinate meetings between researchers and government officials, organize fieldwork, and reach out for funding. It takes field workers who are willing to give up the comforts of home to go out and gather information. It also takes lab researchers like Dr. Manuela who dedicate most of their time to analyzing data, researching new project opportunities, and publishing results for the scientific community.

While you may eventually get to snorkel with wild California sea lions, much of a wildlife researcher's time is spent planning, fundraising, processing data, and writing scientific reports. Researchers study for many years in school, usually earning degrees in biology or zoology. They may also need to travel and work odd hours.

If you're interested in pursuing a career in wildlife research, talk to your parents about visiting local natural history museums, zoos and aquariums, botanical gardens, and wilderness reserves. Consider attending summer camps at these places and participating in science-based activities.

Pay close attention during science classes, especially in biology, and spend your free time learning about and experiencing the world around you. Once you're in high school or college, volunteer at a research lab to get some hands-on experience.

Most importantly, remember that to be a researcher means to never stop asking questions and looking for answers. The answers you find as a wildlife researcher could someday save an endangered species or a threatened habitat that needs your help.

A zoologist from the Laboratory of Medical Zoology collects samples from a natural habitat.
Courtesy of Stephen M. Rich, Laboratory of Medical Zoology

7

CONSERVATION WARRIORS

For Dr. Sharon Hall, an associate professor of ecology, evolution, and environmental science at Arizona State University, a chance encounter with an endangered species helps keep her motivated every day on the job. One summer, Dr. Sharon was studying the impacts of **slash-and-burn agriculture** in the tropical rain forests of Borneo, an island in southeast Asia.

She describes what happened: "One day, I was walking in the forest and heard a rustling in the trees above me. I looked up to see a baby Bornean orangutan that had come down from the treetops to see what I was doing. The baby and I watched each other for what seemed like a very long time—me, sitting down on the ground, and her, moving from branch to branch among the leaves. It seemed like we were getting to know each other quietly, with the bird songs of the rain forest all around us. I have never forgotten that moment."

For Dr. Sharon, this memory is bittersweet. The baby orangutan she encountered that day could be part of one of the last generations of its species to live

Threatened species across the globe rely on zoologists just like you.
Courtesy of BJ Kirschhoffer / polarbearsinternational.org

in the wild. Because humans are destroying orangutans' homes, the rain forests of Borneo and Sumatra, at an alarming rate, the number of orangutans living in their natural habitat has dwindled.

The rain forests of Borneo and Sumatra are being destroyed to provide humans with valuable goods, such as lumber and palm oil. Humans use lumber to build furniture, shipping crates, cabinets, and frames for doors and windows. Some of the wood even ends up as paper.

Palm oil is a common ingredient in products you and your family might buy every day, including baked goods, candy, and many other items you can find in the supermarket. If zoologists and other scientists don't take a stand against

Dr. Sharon Hall takes soil samples in Nepal as part of a conservation project.
Courtesy of Dr. Sharon Hall

the destruction of rain forests, some researchers believe orangutans and other species that live in these areas could become extinct in our lifetime.

For Dr. Sharon, the few minutes she spent with an endangered species on a summer afternoon have pushed her to work hard as an educator and as a scientist. Dr. Sharon's job title may be "professor," but she is one of many zoologists whose ultimate goal is to conserve the natural places that humans and nonhumans call home.

Wildlife cannot survive without a healthy ecosystem, and Dr. Sharon knows a healthy ecosystem begins with healthy soils, plants, water, and air. Through her work, Dr. Sharon helps others understand all the different ways the natural world needs our protection. She is a conservation warrior.

Ecosystems in Trouble

Can you imagine a world without tropical rain forests? If there were no rain forests, orangutans are not the only species that would be in trouble. Humans may have accomplished many great feats, such as traveling to outer space and discovering cures for deadly diseases, but we have also caused great harm to our planet and its environment.

An environmental problem is an undesirable change in the environment, such as air pollution, water pollution, and **deforestation**. One environmental problem zoologists pay close attention to is habitat loss. When humans cut down trees to make way for homes or agriculture like the oil palm plantations from which we get palm oil, animals that live in these habitats must move or die. Even though human survival depends on our ability to use the planet's natural resources, we must do so responsibly.

The giant panda is another example of a species suffering from habitat loss. Destruction of the giant panda's habitat, China's bamboo forests, has made it more difficult for these animals to find the food and shelter they need to survive. Deforestation has also isolated giant pandas from each other, making it more difficult for them to mate and reproduce naturally.

Pollution caused by human activities can also destroy habitats. Accidents, such as an oil spill in the ocean, can badly damage an ecosystem and everything that lives there. Humans' everyday actions can also accumulate and cause big problems. By burning fuel and cutting down forests, humans are adding gases such as carbon dioxide to Earth's **atmosphere**. These gases get trapped as part of the **greenhouse effect**, a natural process that keeps the planet warm. However, as we continue to add gases to our atmosphere, the greenhouse effect intensifies, trapping more heat and causing Earth's global temperatures to rise.

Many scientists believe this phenomenon, called **global warming**, is causing changes in Earth's climate. In the polar regions, warmer temperatures are already having a negative impact. Arctic species like the polar bear are facing new hardships as warmer temperatures melt the region's sea ice, which many species depend on to survive. Unfortunately, these new hardships sometimes result in species decline or even extinction.

Ecologists use the acronym HIPPO to remember five of the most important reasons for today's high levels of species decline and extinction. HIPPO stands for Habitat loss, **Invasive species**, Pollution, Population growth, and Overuse of resources.

Invasive species are organisms that are living in a place they are not supposed to be. In each ecosystem, there are built-in population controls like predators and a limited supply of resources such as food, water, and space. If a species is taken from its native ecosystem and put into a different one, it can create an imbalance. In its new environment, an invasive species may not have any natural predators, so its population numbers could soar as it preys on native species.

Scientists believe global warming is causing sea ice in the Arctic to melt. This is really bad news for polar bears and other species that depend on the sea ice to survive.
Courtesy of Steven C. Amstrup / polarbearsinternational.org

A Warning from Easter Island

There is a small, remote island in the Pacific Ocean that holds dark secrets about its past. Once the backdrop for a thriving society and culture, today's Easter Island is best known for its *moai*, giant statues carved from volcanic rock by its ancient inhabitants. But at what cost did this society thrive?

Archaeologists believe Easter Island was once a tropical oasis filled with many species of trees and birds. However, between AD 400 and 1700, the Polynesians who settled on Easter Island nearly destroyed its natural environment, in large part by cutting down the island's palm forests. When European explorers came upon the island in the 1700s, they reported a near-barren landscape with a greatly diminished human population.

Could the islanders' irresponsible use of their natural resources be to blame for their downfall? While many questions remain about exactly what happened on Easter Island between AD 400 and 1700, deforestation most likely contributed to the civilization's troubles. Like Easter Island, Planet Earth has limited natural resources that all of its inhabitants depend on to survive. If we do not use these resources carefully, we could damage our environment to the point of no return.

The North American bullfrog is one invasive species that has caused trouble across North America and on other continents where it has been introduced. In their natural habitat, bullfrogs help keep insect populations in check thanks to their hefty appetites. In areas like the western United States where they are not native, North American bullfrogs compete with native species, such as other frogs, for food. In some cases, the invasive bullfrog is driving these native species into decline.

Sometimes, pet owners accidentally create problems by releasing nonnative animals into the wild. Burmese pythons, large snakes from southeast Asia that are often bought and sold as pets, have wreaked havoc in the Florida Everglades by preying on the ecosystem's native species. Since there are few natural predators in the Everglades for these gigantic snakes, pythons that have escaped or been released into the park have thrived at the expense of native wildlife.

To stop invasive species from disturbing the balance of local ecosystems, scientists and government workers may work together to introduce natural predators into an area that will help control a "pest" population. These conservation warriors may also educate the public about the dangers of keeping exotic pets and/or releasing them into the wild. By preventing the spread of invasive species, conservation-minded zoologists hope to protect ecosystems, to prevent species decline and extinction, and to preserve biodiversity.

Solving Environmental Problems

In some cases, government officials help conservation efforts by setting public land aside for national parks or nature preserves that protect wild places and the wildlife living in them. Park rangers, ecologists, and other staff work together to keep these areas in good shape for the wildlife and the people who visit.

Lawmakers and politicians may also play a role in conservation by creating rules that protect

CONSERVATION SCIENTIST

Dr. Steven Amstrup

Chief Scientist
Polar Bears International, Bozeman, Montana

"These days, many seem to think humans are merely observers of ecology. In reality, we are participants in it just like all the other creatures out there."

Dr. Steven Amstrup will never forget the time he fell through the roof of a polar bear's den. Suddenly face-to-face with a mother bear and her two small cubs, Dr. Steven could have easily become the family's lunch. Luckily, he lived to tell the tale.

In his past as a wildlife researcher, Dr. Steven spent a lot of time out on the pack ice in the Arctic. Today, he focuses on finding ways to save polar bears from extinction. On a day-to-day basis, this means writing up results from past research projects, planning new projects, collecting outreach/education tools, and working with the media to spread the word: polar bears need our help.

Through interviews, lectures, and other presentations, Dr. Steven plays a key role in communicating the threats to polar bears and what we can do to save them. Dr. Steven hopes to prevent the number of wild polar bears from declining even further, while helping others realize that their actions impact polar bears' future—for better or for worse.

Dr. Steven Amstrup
Courtesy of Steven C. Amstrup /
polarbearsinternational.org

animals and their habitats. One example is placing restrictions on the killing of wildlife, including **poaching**—the illegal hunting or capturing of animals. It's also up to government workers to enforce laws meant to help protect the environment from pollution and other environmentally damaging activities.

Sometimes, lawmaking is not enough to prevent the destruction of an ecosystem or the decline of a species. In these cases, zoologists called wildlife managers step in to help by monitoring a species' population numbers in the wild, by studying its role in its ecosystem, and by implementing strategies to ensure its survival.

Wildlife managers often work for local governments or national government agencies such as the US Fish and Wildlife Service. When there is a problem, like the spread of an invasive species, wildlife managers help find ways to curb the problem and restore a natural balance.

Survive Habitat Loss: The Resource Game

Habitat destruction makes it difficult for animals to find the resources they need to survive. Simulate habitat loss and try to survive as you play the resource game. This activity requires three players and one adult to serve as the moderator.

MATERIALS

- Masking tape or duct tape
- 12 dimes (or any small object)
- 12 nickels (or any small object)
- Pen or black marker
- 9 index cards
- Dice

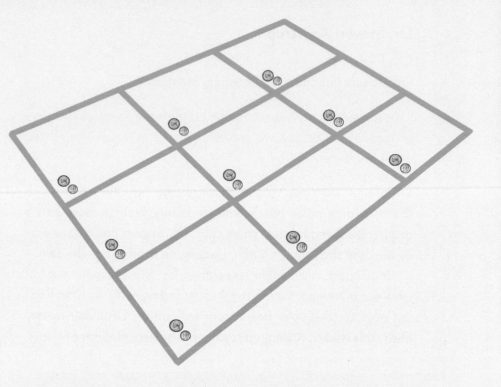

Objective

Stay alive as long as possible as your resources dwindle and your habitat gets smaller.

Set up

Use masking tape or duct tape to create a large square on the ground. With more tape, divide the square into three equally spaced rows and columns, creating nine smaller squares, or "habitats," each large enough for a player to stand in.

Place one dime and one nickel in each habitat square. The dimes represent water resource tokens and the nickels represent food resource tokens. Set the extra tokens aside in case you need them later.

Use a pen or a black marker to write a big *X* on nine index cards. During the game, the moderator will add one of these *X* cards to any habitat square that gets destroyed.

If you're a player, choose an animal species you'd like to represent. Select one of the nine habitat squares and stand inside it. If you're the moderator, read the "How to Play" and "Additional Rules" sections before you start the game.

How to Play

Begin the game by rolling the dice. Read the action below that matches the number you rolled out loud to the players, then follow the directions:

1. Explore a new territory. Each player must move to a new habitat square.

2. Your habitat's water source has been polluted. Each player must give up one water resource token to the moderator.

3. A lumber company has flattened part of this area. The moderator must destroy two habitat squares and remove the resource tokens from those squares.

4. An invasive species has entered your ecosystem, providing new competition for food. Each player must give up one food resource token to the moderator.

5. A natural disaster just hit. The moderator must destroy one habitat square and remove the resource tokens from that square.

6. A conservationist helped restore this area. The moderator can add one habitat square back to the playing field by removing the X card and by restoring one food and one water resource token to the square. (If no habitat squares have been destroyed, each player can choose one resource token to add to his or her square.)

Additional Rules

Only one player can stand in a habitat square at a time. If a player doesn't have the resource token needed to complete a turn, he or she must move to a habitat square that does.

If no open squares have the resource token a player needs to complete the turn, the species becomes extinct; the player must leave the game. If two players try to claim the same habitat square, the first one there survives.

To destroy a habitat, the moderator adds an X card to the square and removes its resource tokens. Players cannot live in a habitat that has been destroyed. The moderator can destroy whichever habitat he or she wants, including those in which a player is standing. If a player is standing in a habitat that's being destroyed, he or she must move to a different open square. If there is no open square, the player is eliminated.

The game ends when there is only one player left on the board or when all remaining players are eliminated. See how long your group can go before all three species become extinct!

Scientists at universities, including professors and students, also help conservation efforts by researching environmental problems and coming up with solutions. As an environmental scientist at a university, Dr. Sharon works closely with students in her classroom, laboratory, and sometimes in the field to teach them how science can be used to address conservation issues.

International organizations, and all the people who work there, also lead and encourage worldwide conservation efforts. The United Nations Environment Programme (UNEP) helps identify global environmental issues and work toward solutions. The International Union for Conservation of Nature and Natural Resources (IUCN) keeps tabs on the world's endangered species and promotes conservation strategies. IUCN's Red List identifies species that are threatened in the wild so scientists around the world can help prevent these species' extinction.

Other important players on the worldwide conservation stage include the people who run fundraising organizations such as World Wildlife Fund and charities such as Durrell Wildlife Conservation Trust. Many of these organizations raise awareness about conservation needs through research and education. Each and every conservation organization relies on an army of conservation warriors to conduct research, to raise money and awareness for a cause, and to communicate with the public, local communities, and local governments.

Polar Bears International is one example of a conservation organization that conducts field

(*left*) Western lowland gorillas are one of hundreds of species protected under an AZA Species Survival Plan. *Courtesy of ZSL London Zoo*

(*right*) Przewalski's horses still exist in the wild thanks to a worldwide effort from conservationists and zoo-led reintroduction programs. *Courtesy of Chicago Zoological Society / Jim Schulz*

research to learn more about how polar bears and other Arctic species are handling climate shifts. The employees and volunteers at Polar Bears International take action by training other conservation leaders, helping communities manage their natural resources, and educating citizens about how they can make a difference.

Many zoos and aquariums also help protect endangered species by making conservation part of their mission statements. These institutions educate the public about conservation needs, they raise money for wildlife charities, they organize conservation projects, and they encourage staff members to help conservation efforts as part of their commitment to the field of zoology.

Zoos and aquariums also participate by breeding endangered species at their facilities. In North America, the Association of Zoos and Aquariums (AZA) has a program called the Species Survival Plan that aims to manage, conserve, and protect more than 500 endangered species, such as the giant panda and the western lowland gorilla. Zoos and aquariums that participate in Species Survival Plans are helping to prevent these species from becoming extinct.

In some cases, zoo-born animals that are part of recovery plans can be reintroduced into the wild. While reintroduction is difficult, there are several success stories involving species such as the Arabian oryx, the California condor, and the Przewalski's horse.

The Przewalski's horse is a wild horse species that once roamed in great numbers across Europe and Asia, particularly in Mongolia. The horse

The Case of the Black-Footed Ferret

Zoologists believed black-footed ferrets were extinct in the wild until a small group turned up in Wyoming during the 1980s. Conservation warriors working in Wyoming's fish and game department, the US Fish and Wildlife Service, and several North American zoos stepped in to help.

To save this species from extinction, these zoologists needed to provide safe places for the ferrets to breed and recover their population numbers. Then, the goal was to release some of the animals back into their natural habitat and reestablish a population of black-footed ferrets in the wild.

Among the zoos that participate in this ongoing reintroduction program is Arizona's Phoenix Zoo. Stuart Wells, the director of conservation and science at Phoenix Zoo, was part of the team of conservationists that started the zoo's black-footed ferret program. Stuart had already worked in conservation for much of his career, helping to develop a breeding program for endangered cheetahs and working with the US Fish and Wildlife Service on endangered species conservation. However, he says the most memorable moment of his career so far was the first time he released a black-footed ferret back into the wild.

A zoologist's ability to be involved in a species' survival is one example of how fulfilling a career in conservation can be. Today, thanks to conservation warriors like Stuart and many others across North America, there are an estimated 500 to 1,000 black-footed ferrets living in the wild, and the number is growing.

Black-footed ferrets were once thought to be extinct in the wild.
Courtesy of Phoenix Zoo

became extinct in the wild by the 1960s, partly as a result of hunting and habitat destruction. Since the only remaining Przewalski's horses lived in zoos, these institutions worked together to breed the animals and reintroduce some of them into the wild. Thanks to these efforts, there are Przewalski's horses roaming Mongolia once more. Hopefully one day, the species will thrive in its natural habitat without our help.

Getting a Job

Conservation warriors are a diverse bunch. This is because *conservationist* is less of a job title and more of a broad term for people who contribute to conservation in some way or another. Zoologists like Dr. Sharon, who works at a university; Dr. Steven, who works at Polar Bears International; and Stuart, who works at Phoenix Zoo, are all conservationists.

Conservation warriors also include wildlife managers, park rangers, conservation-minded lawmakers and politicians, and many of the other people you've read about in this book. Think about all the zookeepers, aquarists, and other zoo crew who work every day to share what they know about animals with the public. Think about all the veterinarians who volunteer their services to help injured wildlife or who travel across the world to participate in field research. Also think about all the wildlife researchers who collect and analyze the data needed to determine what the problems are. These people are all conservationists, too.

To become a conservation warrior, think about what you like to do. What are you good at?

Chances are, there's a way to use your skills to make a difference. It's true—anyone who uses his or her skills to address an environmental problem or help a conservation effort can be a conservationist. Imagine how many jobs this could include!

Do you like to read and write? You could become a writer who works for an environmental agency, a conservation organization, a zoo or aquarium, or even a magazine like *National Geographic* or *Smithsonian* that covers new scientific discoveries in the animal kingdom, as well as environmental and conservation issues.

Do you like taking photographs? You could be a conservation warrior by becoming a wildlife photographer. By capturing photos that amaze and inspire others, wildlife photographers help connect people with wildlife and the natural world, encouraging them to do their part to preserve Earth's biodiversity.

Educators are significant in the conservation community. Instructors who teach kids like you about zoology are helping to create a generation of conservation-minded individuals. Famous media personalities like Lucy Cooke, Jeff Corwin, Jack Hanna, Steve Irwin, and the Kratt Brothers have all done important work to educate the public about animals. The more people know about the animal kingdom, the more they care about preserving it for their children and grandchildren.

Conservation warriors come into the field of zoology with a wide range of educational backgrounds and expertise. Some of them spend many years in school earning advanced degrees in biology, ecology, environmental science, or zoology.

> "We should preserve every scrap of biodiversity as priceless while we learn to use it and come to understand what it means to humanity."
> —Edward O. Wilson, biologist, researcher, professor, author

Make an Endangered Species Flyer

You're a writer who works for a conservation organization like Polar Bears International. Your latest assignment is to create a flyer about an endangered species that your coworkers can hand out at an upcoming event. This activity requires access to the Internet or a library.

MATERIALS

- Pen or pencil and paper
- Photo of an endangered animal
- Scissors
- 8½-inch-by-11-inch sheet of paper or poster board
- Glue stick or other adhesive
- Markers

Begin by choosing an endangered species you'd like to learn more about. A good place to start might be the IUCN's Red List (http://discover .iucnredlist.org).

Research the animal you've selected by searching for facts on the Internet, in an animal reference book, or in an encyclopedia. Write down the animal's scientific name and what it eats in the wild.

Next, research the animal's natural habitat. In which biome can this species be found? Also write down the global region where the animal lives, such as South America, eastern Asia, or the coastal waters off Australia.

Now, determine the animal's status in the wild. If possible, find some information about how many individuals from your species are still living in the wild and how this number has changed from the past.

Try your best to find out why this species is endangered. For instance, is your animal losing its habitat like orangutans and giant pandas are? Is climate change or pollution making it difficult for your animal to survive?

In your own words, write a paragraph on a spare piece of paper (or type it on a computer) that summarizes your research. You could write one sentence that introduces your animal and talks about what it eats, another sentence about where it can be found in the wild, and a few more sentences about why it is endangered.

Find a photo of your animal that you can print from the Internet or photocopy from a book. Cut it out and set it aside.

Begin designing your flyer by writing the animal's name in big, bold letters at the top of a sheet of paper or poster board. Add the animal's scientific name underneath in smaller letters. Paste the photo wherever you'd like.

Neatly copy your paragraph onto the flyer. Or, if you've typed the information, print it out and paste it on. Use markers to spruce your flyer up with some color or hand-drawn decorations.

Extra Credit

Pretend you are a teacher giving a lesson about this endangered species. Present the information on your flyer to friends or family members, along with some ideas to save this species from extinction.

Interview a Zoologist

Want to know what it's really like to be a zoologist? One of the best ways to find out is to ask one.

MATERIALS

- Pen or pencil
- Notebook

> ### Tip
>
> *If you can't get in touch with a zoologist, simply sit down and brainstorm what you've learned by reading Zoology for Kids. Which was your favorite chapter? Who was your favorite zoologist? Next, come up with a plan to begin your own journey as a zoologist.*

Which career piqued your interest the most as you read through this book? Brainstorm with an adult about how you could talk to a real-life zoologist. If you live by a zoo or aquarium, that might be a good place to start.

Next, think about what you'd like to know, then write down some questions to ask your zoologist. Make sure to include the questions "How can I make a difference?" and "What can I do now to start my zoology career?"

Ask an adult to help you coordinate your interview. Depending on the situation, it might be best to conduct the interview in person, on the phone, or via e-mail. Be sure to take notes if you conduct your interview in person or on the telephone.

After the interview, sit down with a parent, guardian, or teacher and come up with a plan to participate in the zoology community. This could take many forms. For instance, do you want to stop buying products that contain palm oil? Do you want to take a trip to the local beach or park to pick up trash? Do you want to take a class at a zoo or aquarium to learn more about animals? Do you want to raise some money for a conservation organization by mowing neighbors' lawns, selling lemonade, or coordinating a car wash in your community?

Write your zoologist a thank-you note for his or her time. Include a few sentences in the note that talks about your plan.

Others don't need to pursue as much formal schooling.

To set yourself up for the path that best suits you, talk to a parent, teacher, or career counselor to figure out which classes you should take in school, which activities you should participate in during your free time, and what types of hands-on experience you can gain. Like other careers in zoology, a combination of learning as much as you can in school and finding ways to apply that knowledge in your community is the best strategy.

The Future Is You

As a future zoologist, the first step toward making a difference is acknowledging that humans impact the environment. The next step is to take some responsibility by educating yourself and others about what we can do to preserve the natural world. Remember, whether you choose to become a wildlife photographer, a journalist, a park ranger, a wildlife manager, a zoo curator, an ecology professor, or even a TV show host who spreads the word about conservation, there is a way to use your talents to make a difference.

In the meantime, don't leave conservation up to someone else! Continue to learn about animals, their forms, functions, and cool behaviors, as well as how they interact with each other and with their environments. Support a zoo or aquarium by buying an admission ticket, or organize a fundraiser and donate your earnings to a wildlife research or conservation organization. Finally, search for ways your family can make less of an impact on the environment, which can help save threatened species like the polar bear.

No matter what you're good at, you can help solve today's toughest conservation issues, and you can start in your very own backyard. The field of zoology needs passionate young people with all sorts of talents who are willing to work hard and dream big. If you believe in a world where humans respect, admire, and protect the animal kingdom, the field of zoology needs you.

ACKNOWLEDGMENTS

This book wouldn't have been possible without the overwhelming love and support of fellow zoologists from around the world. Special thanks to Mike Adkesson, Steven Amstrup and Polar Bears International, Renée Friedman, Mark Gonka, Manuela González-Suárez, Barron Hall, Liesl Pimentel, Miguel Pinto, Daniela Schmieder, Denise Wagner, and many others who shared expert knowledge, photos, or advice. A grateful shout-out to Brookfield Zoo, Phoenix Zoo, Shedd Aquarium, Tampa's Lowry Park Zoo, Woodland Park Zoo, and ZSL London Zoo for donating amazing photos.

Thanks also to Lisa Reardon, who was our project's first fan, and to the Kratt Brothers, who have inspired so many young zoologists to do what they love—including us! Cheers to our talented illustrator, Bryce, and to our enthusiastic activity testers: Karis, Naomi, Anna-Grace, Jayden, Easton, Logan, Madyson, and Tannen.

Authors Josh and Bethanie Hestermann with Martin and Chris Kratt.
Courtesy of Chicago Zoological Society / Jim Schulz

GLOSSARY

altruism: In zoology, when an animal behaves in a way that benefits another animal, even if it harms itself in the process.

anesthesia: Medicine that reduces or eliminates pain, often used during surgery to put a patient into a state of unconsciousness.

animal husbandry: In zoology, the care of animals and their physical, mental, and emotional well-being.

antibodies: Proteins produced by an animal's body that defend against invaders such as bacteria and viruses.

apex predator: An animal at the top of its food chain, with few or no natural predators in its ecosystem.

artifact: Any item made by a human being.

atmosphere: The mass of gases that surrounds a planet.

biodiversity: The diversity, or variety, of plant and animal life on Earth.

bioluminescence: The production of light without creating heat by organisms such as fireflies.

biome: A collection of ecosystems on Earth that share a similar climate and pattern of vegetation.

breeding: The process of producing offspring or young.

camouflage: The result of an animal's form, coloring, patterning, or behavior that helps it avoid unwanted attention by blending in, appearing to be something it's not, or otherwise confusing predators.

cells: Microscopic structures that serve as the basic building blocks of life.

census: A count or survey of a population.

climate: Typical weather conditions in a specific area.

cold blooded (ectothermic): Refers to animals, such as reptiles and insects, whose body temperatures change along with the temperature of their environments.

commensalism: A relationship between different organisms within an ecosystem in which one organism benefits and the other isn't affected.

community: A group of animals of different species interacting in the same time and place.

conservation: The attempt to preserve, restore, manage, or maintain a natural balance within an ecosystem.

consumer: An organism that eats other organisms, living or dead. In a food chain, primary consumers eat producers, secondary consumers eat primary consumers, and so on.

data: Facts, statistics, or other information for studying or referencing.

decomposer: An organism that gains energy by breaking down the remains of dead organisms, recycling nutrients back into the ecosystem.

deforestation: The removal of trees from a habitat.

echolocation: An animal's ability to locate objects such as predators and prey using reflected sounds or echoes.

ecology: The study of organisms' interactions with one another and with their environments.

ecosystem: A natural unit made up of plants, animals, and their environments.

endangered species: A threatened species with limited numbers left in the wild.

enrichment: The process of adding means for mental and/or physical stimulation to an animal's environment, providing it with more choices and the chance to display natural behaviors.

ethogram: A catalog of an animal's behaviors.

evidence: Available facts and information to help decide whether a belief is true.

evolution: In biology, the process by which a species changes throughout time.

extinction: The disappearance of a species from Earth.

focal sample: The record of one animal's behaviors after a period of focused observation.

food chain: A sequence that traces how food energy gets transferred within an ecosystem as organisms eat and are eaten by other organisms.

foraging: Animal behavior associated with searching for, finding, and eating food.

fossils: Preserved traces or remains of organisms from the past.

global warming: A gradual temperature increase in Earth's atmosphere and oceans resulting from air pollution that traps heat as part of the greenhouse effect.

greenhouse effect: The result of Earth's atmosphere trapping heat from the sun, which is necessary for life on the planet.

habitat: An area within an ecosystem where an organism, a population, or a community lives.

hibernation: A winter survival strategy in which an animal enters a state of inactivity and uses minimal energy.

hypothesis: A possible answer to a scientific question that can be tested by conducting an experiment or by gathering observations of the natural world.

infectious diseases: Illnesses caused by organisms such as bacteria, viruses, fungi, or parasites entering the body.

innate: Refers to unlearned behavior that can be performed for the first time without practice.

invasive species: A disruptive organism living in an environment where it is not native.

keystone species: A species that plays a major role in its ecosystem.

metamorphosis: The process by which an animal's form, function, and behavior change as it transforms into an adult, such as when a tadpole develops into a frog.

migration: The seasonal movement of animals between two places.

mobility: The ability to move around freely.

mutualism: A win-win relationship between different organisms within an ecosystem in which each organism benefits from the arrangement.

parasitism: A relationship between different organisms within an ecosystem in which one organism benefits by harming another organism.

photosynthesis: A process by which producers capture energy from the sun and transform it into energy they can use.

pigment: A substance that gives color to an organism's tissue.

poaching: The illegal hunting or capturing of animals.

pollination: The transfer of pollen among plants, which allows the plants to reproduce.

population: In ecology, a group of organisms living in the same time and place that are part of the same species.

positive reinforcement: A training method by which something is added to an animal's environment after a behavior that makes that behavior more likely to happen again.

predation: The interaction between a predator and its prey.

predator: An organism that captures another organism for food.

prey: An organism that is captured for food.

producer: In ecology, an organism at the bottom of a food chain that gains energy from its physical environment, including the sun.

scavenger: A type of consumer that feeds on dead or dying matter.

scientific method: A procedure used by scientists to test hypotheses and find answers to scientific questions.

scientific name: A formal Latin name given to each organism, usually printed in italics.

slash-and-burn agriculture: A technique in which land is cleared by cutting and burning existing vegetation for farming.

tissue: In biology, specialized collections of cells that make up the material of which animals are made.

warm blooded (endothermic): Refers to animals, including most birds and mammals, that can maintain a stable body temperature even when the temperature of their environments change.

zoology: A branch of biology that focuses on the study of animal life.

zoonotic disease: A disease that can be transmitted from a nonhuman animal to a human being.

RESOURCES

American Association of Zoo Keepers (AAZK)

www.aazk.org

This site is for animal care professionals, but it could be interesting to those who want to join the field some day as a zoologist. Check out the upcoming events and read more about AAZK's conservation fundraisers such as Bowling for Rhinos, an annual bowl-a-thon.

American Veterinary Medical Association (AVMA)

www.avma.org

AVMA's website offers information for current veterinarians, aspiring vets and vet techs, and K–12 educators planning lessons on what it's like to be part of this exciting field.

Association of Zoos and Aquariums (AZA)

www.aza.org

For the latest news in the world of zoos and aquariums, turn to AZA's website, which highlights everything from animal births to conservation efforts. Use this site to find AZA-accredited zoos or aquariums near you.

Duke Lemur Center

http://lemur.duke.edu

If you love lemurs, this is a site for you. Meet the lemurs living at this important research center, and if you feel led to lend a helping hand, you can even "adopt" one!

Durrell Wildlife Conservation Trust

www.durrell.org

Durrell Wildlife Conservation Trust is a conservation organization dedicated to preventing species extinctions. Learn about endangered species, threatened habitats, and most importantly, what you can do to help.

International Union for Conservation of Nature (IUCN)

www.iucn.org; http://discover.iucnredlist.org

IUCN is a great resource for learning about environmental problems, worldwide conservation efforts, and endangered species.

Laboratory of Medical Zoology at the University of Massachusetts

www.tickdiseases.org

This is a good example of a place where lab researchers work.

National Geographic Animals

www.nationalgeographic.com/animals

This site has a wealth of information on different animal species. Use it as a resource for many of the activities in this book.

Orangutan Outreach

www.redapes.org

Learn more about orangutans, habitat loss, and what you can do to help.

Polar Bears International

www.polarbearsinternational.org

Polar Bears International is a go-to site for teachers and students who want to learn more about polar bears and climate change.

US Fish and Wildlife Service Endangered Species

www.fws.gov/endangered

If you live in the United States, go to this site to search for endangered species in your state. Read about species recovery plans underway throughout the country.

World Association of Zoos and Aquariums (WAZA)

www.waza.org

On the WAZA site, find a list of WAZA-accredited zoos and aquariums, read up on the association's conservation efforts, and keep up to date on industry news.

World Wildlife Fund (WWF)

www.worldwildlife.org

Learn more about what the public can do to preserve and protect the natural world. The site profiles endangered species, endangered habitats, and ecological threats to the environment, including pollution and deforestation.

SELECTED BIBLIOGRAPHY

Suitable for young readers.

Alcock, John. *Animal Behavior.* 8th ed. Sunderland, MA: Sinauer Associates, 2005.

Allaby, Michael, ed. *A Dictionary of Zoology.* 2nd ed. Oxford: Oxford University Press, 1999.

Alters, Sandra. *Biology: Understanding Life.* St. Louis: Mosby-Year Book, 1996.

Baratay, Eric, and Elisabeth Hardouin-Fugier. *Zoo: A History of Zoological Gardens in the West.* Trans. Oliver Welsh. London: Reaktion Books, 2002.

Brennan, Scott, and Jay Withgott. *Environment: The Science behind the Stories.* San Francisco: Pearson Education, 2005.

*Burnie, David, and Don Wilson. *Animal.* 3rd ed. London: Dorling Kindersley, 2011.

Domjan, Michael. *The Principles of Learning and Behavior.* 5th ed. Belmont, CA: Wadsworth, 2003.

Encyclopædia Britannica Online Academic Edition. Encyclopædia Britannica Inc. Web. www.britannica.com.

Gordon, Malcolm, and Soraya Bartol, eds. *Experimental Approaches to Conservation Biology.* Berkeley: University of California Press, 2004.

Harris, C. Leon. *Concepts in Zoology.* 2nd ed. New York: HarperCollins, 1996.

Hickman, Cleveland, Larry Roberts, and Allan Larson. *Integrated Principles of Zoology.* 11th ed. New York: McGraw-Hill, 2001.

*Irwin, Steve, and Terri Irwin. *The Crocodile Hunter: The Incredible Life and Adventures of Steve and Terri Irwin.* New York: Dutton, 2001.

Kahn, Cynthia. *The Merck Veterinary Manual.* 10th ed. Whitehouse Station, NJ: Merck & Co., 2010.

Karesh, William. *Appointment at the Ends of the World.* New York: Warner Books, 1999.

Kisling, Vernon. *Zoo and Aquarium History: Ancient Animal Collection to Zoological Gardens.* Boca Raton, FL: CRC Press, 2001.

Miller, Stephen, and John Harley. *Zoology.* 6th ed. New York: McGraw-Hill, 2005.

*O'Toole, Christopher. *Firefly Encyclopedia of Insects and Spiders.* Toronto: Firefly Books, 2002.

Pliny the Elder. *Natural History: A Selection.* Trans. John Healy. London: Penguin Books, 1991.

Rees, Paul. *An Introduction to Zoo Biology and Management.* Chichester, England: Wiley-Blackwell, 2011.

*Reis, Ronald. *Easter Island.* New York: Infobase Learning, 2012.

Starr, Cecie. *Biology: Concepts and Applications.* 2nd ed. Belmont, CA: Wadsworth, 1994.

Wright, R. Gerald. *Wildlife Research and Management in the National Parks.* Urbana: University of Illinois Press, 1992.

Young, Robert. *Environmental Enrichment for Captive Animals.* Oxford: Blackwell Publishing, 2003.

INDEX

Page numbers in *italics* indicate pictures

A

Adkesson, Dr. Mike, *68*, *69–70*, *79*
African crested porcupine, *19*, *53*
African elephant, *4*, *14*
African wild dogs, 30
Alexander the Great, 9
altruism, 31, 44
Amstrup, Dr. Steven, 105, *105*
anemone, *2*, 13, *55*, 98
anesthesia, 71, 74
animal cell cake (activity), 11–12
animal cells, 8, 10
animal husbandry, *55–56*, 64
animal training, 58, 60, 61

animals, defined, 8
antelopes, *19*, 30
antibodies, *77*, 80
antlers, 19, *19*
apex predators, 46
Apps for Apes, 58
aquarists, 54–56, 66–67
aquariums, 54, 61, 63–64, 66–67, 109
aquatic biomes, 47
archaeologists, 14, 104
Arctic foxes, 21
Aristotle, 5, 9, 97
armadillos, 19
artifacts, 14
Association of Zoos and Aquariums (AZA), 64, 109
aye-ayes, *24*, *25–26*, *26*

B

background matching, 20
backyard zoology (activity), *95*
baking, 11–12
bats, 17, 31, 44, 45, 81
bears, 28, 33, *33*, 43
beetles, 13, 20, *36*
behavioral enrichment, 58
behavioral enrichment (activity), 59
behaviors, 25–37, 58–63
binomial nomenclature, 97
biodiversity, 47, 104, 110
bioluminescence, 36–37, *37*
biomes, 47

Bird Island, 85–86, *86*

birds, 8, 17, 20, 26, *26*, 28, 30, *33*, 44

birds of paradise, *33*

births, 31–32, 70, 81

black-footed ferrets, 109, *109*

blubber, 17

Borneo, 101, 102

bridges (training technique), 61, 62

Brookfield Zoo, *69. See also* Chicago Zoological Society

bullfrogs, 104

butterflies, 13, *33, 116*

butterfly life cycle (activity), 34–35

C

Caldwell, Bridget, *53*

camouflage, 7–8, 20–22

canine distemper, 80–81

Cárdenas-Alayza, Susana, 87

careers

   about, 2–3, 112

   conservation warriors, 110, 113

   researchers, 85–87, 92, 93–94, 99

   veterinarians, 67, 69–71, 74–77, 83

   veterinary technicians, 74

   zookeepers and aquarists, 53–56, 64, 66–67

carnivores, 46, 96

cartilage, 13

cattle egrets, 44

cells, 8, 10, *10*

census, 86, 93

chameleons, 23, *23*

cheetahs, 74

Chicago Zoological Society, 87

chromosomes, 10

chuckwallas, 27, *27, 63*

cichlids, 32

claws, 20

climates, 47

cognitive enrichment, 58

cold blooded, 17

colors, 23, *23*

commensalism, 44

communication, 32–33

communities, 43–44

concealing coloration, 20–21

concealing coloration (activity), 22

conservation efforts, 96, 99, 104–105, 108–109

conservation scientists, 105

conservation warriors, 110

consumers, 8, 46

Cooke, Lucy, 110

copycats, 21, 23

Corwin, Jeff, *93*, 110

crickets, *36*

curators, 67

cuttlefish, 6, 7–8, *8*, 20–21

cytoplasm, 10, *10*

D

Darwin, Charles, 64

deciduous forests, 47

decomposers, 41, 46

deep sea communication (activity), 38–39

deforestation, 102–103

dental procedures, 71

dependent variables, 88

deserts, 47

digging for bones (activity), 15–16

direction, sense of (activity), 29

discovery (in research), 94, 96

disguises, 21

dolphin echolocation game (activity), 18

ducks, *x*

E

Easter Island, 104
echolocation, 17
echolocation game (activity), 18
ecology, 3, 42–43
ecosystems, 44, 46–47
education, 64, 66–67, 99
El Niño, 87
elephants, 4, 14, 31, 60, 74
Emperor penguins, 28, *28*
endangered species, 96, 101–102, 108–109. *See also* conservation efforts
endangered species flyer (activity), 111
endoplasmic reticula, 10
endoskeletons, 13
enrichment, 56–58, 66
environment, 43, 87, 102, 104–105
ethograms, 93, 94, 95
exhibit planning (activity), 65
exoskeleton, 13

experiment: keeping warm (activity), 90–91
experiments, 88–89
extinction, 92, 103–104, 109
eyelash leaf frogs, 21, *21*

F

families, 28, 32
feathers, 17
ferrets, *71*, 109, *109*
field research, 89, 93
field research (activity), 95
fighting, 30
fireflies, 36
fish, 10, 17, 30, *30*, 37, 44, 55
Flatz, Ramona, *93*
focal samples, 93
food chain, 46, 47
food chain (activity), 48–49
foraging, **25**
fossas, 42, *42*
fossils, 14
foxes, 21
Friedman, Renée, 14
frilled lizards, 36
frogs, *2*, 21, *21*, *75*
fruit bats, 45
fruit salad (activity), 45
fur, 17, 21
fur seals, 87

G

gazelles, 19, *19*
giant Australian cuttlefish, *6*, 7–8, *8*
giant pandas, 103
global warming, 103
González-Suárez, Dr. Manuela, 92, *92*
Goodall, Jane, 51
gorillas, *108*
grapeshot carpet anemone, *2*
grasslands, 47
Great Barrier Reef, 44, 46
greenhouse effect, 103

H

habitat loss survival (activity), 106–107
Hall, Dr. Barron, 74
Hall, Dr. Sharon, 101–102, *102*, 108
Hanna, Jack, 83, 110
herbivores, 46
herds, 30
Hestermann, Josh, *61*
hibernation, 27
Hierakonpolis, 14
HIPPO acronym, 103
hippopotamus, 30
hoofed animals, 19
horns, *19*, 19–20
horses, *108*, 109–110
humans, 8, 13, 32, 43, 46–47, 80
humpback whales, *36*
hydrostatic skeleton, 13
hypotheses, 87–88

I

immune system, 80
independent variables, 88
infectious diseases, 80, 89
inflammation, 80
innate behaviors, 26
intelligence, 27–28
interactions, 43–44
International Union for Conservation of Nature and Natural Resources (IUCN), 108
interview a zoologist (activity), 112
invasive species, 103–104
invent a new species (activity), 98
Irwin, Steve, *63*, 110
Isla San Jorge, 85–86, *86*

J

jawbones, *73*

K

keystone species, 46
koalas, 32, *32*
Kratt, Martin and Chris, 110

L

Laboratory of Medical Zoology at the University of Massachusetts, 89, *89*, *99*
laws, 63, 104–105
learned behaviors, 26
lemurs, 42, *42*
life cycle, 33, 42
light production, 36
Linnaeus, Carolus, 97
lions, *27*
London Zoo, 64

M

macaques, *70*
Mandarin duck, *x*
mantispids, *13*
marine mammals, 10, 17, 28
mating, 30–31, 32
meerkats, *52*, *53*

menageries, 64

metamorphosis, 32, 33

migration, 28

milk snakes, 21, 23

Mitchell, John Rex, 56, *56*

mitochondria, 10

mobility, 8

moose, 19, *19*

Morse, Samuel, 38

Morse code (activity), 38–39

muscles, 13

mutualism, 44

N

naked mole rats, 31

naming a species (activity), 98

naming systems, 97

neighborhoods, 46–47

New Caledonian crows, 28

Newton, Isaac, 43

nocturnal animals, 17, 25

North American bullfrogs, 104

nucleus, 10, *10*

O

observational research, 93, 95

ocelots, 36

octopus, 28

Ok, Steven, 66, *66*

okapis, *47*

olinguitos, 96, *96*

omnivores, 46

Orangutan Outreach, 58

orangutans, 101–102

organelles, 10

organs, 10, 13

owls, 17, *17*, 43

P

paleontologists, 14

paleontology (activity), 15–16

palm oil, 102

pandas, 30, 103

parasitism, 44

parenting, 32

pathogens, 80

penguins, 28, *28*

Phoenix Zoo, 109, 110

photosynthesis, 46

pilot fish, 44

plant cells, 10

plasma membrane, 8, 10

poaching, 105

poison dart frog, *2*

poisonous animals, 20

polar bears, *33*, *33*, *100*, 103, *103*, 105, *105*

Polar Bears International, 105, 108–109, 110

pollination, 44

pollution, 102–103

populations, 43

porcupines, 19

positive reinforcement, 60, 62

predation, 44

predators, *42*, *42*, 44

pregnancy, 31, 81

producers, 8

proteins, 10

Przewalski's horses, *108*, 109–110

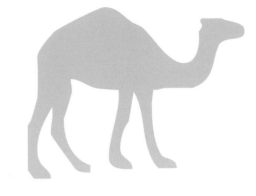

Q

quills, 19

R

rain forests, 47, 102
raptors, 17
red-tailed hawks, *40*, 41
research labs, 88–89
researchers, 85–87, 92, 93–94, 99
resource game (activity), 106–107
rhinoceros, *31*, *50*, 60, 76
ribosomes, 10

S

scanning (behavioral research), 93
scavengers, 46
scent markings, 36
scientific method, 87
scientific names, 97
screech owls, *17*
scutes, 19
sea jellies, *37*
sea lions, 61, *84*, 85–86, 93–94

sea otters, 28, 46, *46*
seahorses, 31, *32*
sense of direction (activity), 29
senses, 17
sharks, 13, 17, 44, 56
Shedd Aquarium, 56
skeletons, 13
slash-and-burn agriculture, 101
snakes, 21, 23
social behavior, 28, 30
social enrichment, 58
Solomon Island leaf frog, 21
species' survival, 109
spines, 19
stethoscopes (activity), 78–79
structural tissues, 13
Sumatra, 102
survival tools, 14, 17
Swenson, Dr. Julie, 76, *76*
symmetry, 13

T

taigas, 47
talons, 20
Tantor (elephant), 74
targeting (training technique), 61
teaching zoos, 66
temperature, body, 17, 27, 90–91
termites, 30
tiger teeth (activity), 72–73, *73*
tissues, 10, 13
tools, 28
Tower of London, 64
toxins, 20
train your friends (activity), 62
training animals, 58, 60, 61
tropical climates, 47
tusks, 20

U

United Nations Environment Programme
(UNEP), 108

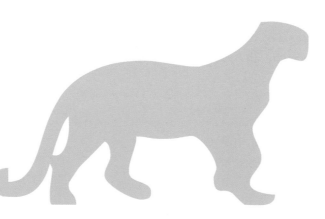

V

vampire bats, 31
venomous animals, 20
veterinarians, 67, 69–71, 74–77, 83
veterinary dentists, 72
veterinary technicians, 74
vital signs (activity), 82
volunteers, 67

W

walking sticks, 21, *21*
walruses, 20
warm blooded, 17
waxy monkey frogs, *75*
Wells, Stuart, 109
Western lowland gorillas, *108*
whales, 36
wildlife managers, 105
Wilson, Edward O., 110
winter sleep, 27–28

Z

zebras, 20, *20*
zoo meals, 57–58
zookeepers, 53–56, 64, 66–67
zoologist interview (activity), 112
zoology, defined, 1
zoonotic diseases, 81, 89
zoos
    about, 54, 56–58
    conservation efforts, 109
    education programs, 61, 63, 67
    exhibit design, 63–64
    history, 64

$14.95 (CAN $16.95)
978-1-56976-807-5
Also available in e-book formats
Ages 9 & up

Awesome Snake Science!
40 Activities for Learning About Snakes

Cindy Blobaum

"This book goes a long way to helping the average student understand reptiles and support their interests. The simulations, models, and facts will be appreciated by both young readers and their teachers." —National Science Teachers Association

"The variety, originality, and ease of most of the activities assure satisfied readers and repeated use." —*School Library Journal*

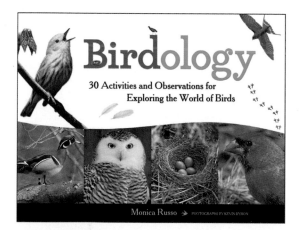

$15.95 (CAN $18.95)
978-1-61374-949-4
Also available in e-book formats
Ages 7 & up

Birdology
30 Activities and Observations for Exploring the World of Birds

Monica Russo; photographs by Kevin Byron

"*Birdology* is a great introduction to the world of birds, featuring a wealth of activities and engaging information." —Bill Grabin, president, York County Audubon Society

"*Birdology* is filled with facts that educate seasoned birders and activities that welcome new observers. Regardless of where one lives, from city streets to rural countryside to the shoreline, teachers and families will find ideas for easily introducing children to nature." —Bernie Alie, youth services librarian, Kennebunk Free Library, Kennebunk, Maine

$14.95 (CAN $16.95)
978-1-55652-568-1
Also available in e-book formats
Ages 7 & up

Insectigations
40 Hands-On Activities to Explore the Insect World

Cindy Blobaum

"Clearly written and well organized . . . will appeal both to budding young scientists and teachers hunting for imaginative lesson-plan ideas." —*School Library Journal*

"Delightful. . . . Connects kids directly to hands-on experience with wild things—exactly what we need more of!" —Jim Pease, PhD, Extension Wildlife Specialist, Natural Resource Ecology and Management Department, Iowa State University

Available at your favorite bookstore, by calling (800) 888-4741, or at www.chicagoreviewpress.com